Aging, Ageism and Abuse: Moving from Awareness to Action

Aging, Ageism and Abuse: Moving from Awareness to Action

Edited by

Gloria Gutman and Charmaine Spencer

ELSEVIER

AMSTERDAM • BOSTON • HEIDELBERG • LONDON • NEW YORK • OXFORD
PARIS • SAN DIEGO • SAN FRANCISCO • SINGAPORE • SYDNEY • TOKYO

Elsevier
32 Jamestown Road London NW1 7BY
30 Corporate Drive, Suite 400, Burlington, MA 01803, USA

First edition 2010

British Library Cataloguing in Publication Data
A catalogue record for this book is available from the British Library

Library of Congress Cataloging-in-Publication Data
A catalog record for this book is available from the Library of Congress

ISBN: 978-0-12-381508-8

Transferred to Digital Printing in 2010

For information on all Elsevier publications
visit our website at elsevierdirect.com

This book has been manufactured using Print On Demand technology. Each copy is produced to order and is limited to black ink. The online version of this book will show colour figures where appropriate.

Contents

Preface

Gloria Gutman, Charmaine Spencer

In developing this book, we had three main objectives: (1) to underscore the important of recognizing and addressing the ageism that underlies much of the abuse and neglect of older persons that is taking place around the world; (2) to draw attention to the diversity of those who are victims and perpetrators of elder abuse and neglect; and (3) to highlight the need to move beyond raising awareness to taking action on the policy level as well as "on the ground" and to providing some examples that it is occurring.

The idea for this volume originated at a conference by the same title held at Simon Fraser University, Vancouver, British Columbia, May 11–12, 2006. The conference was the first activity in the province leading up to the first-ever World Elder Abuse Awareness Day, which took place on June 15, 2006. The conference organizers, Gloria Gutman and Charmaine Spencer, who are also the editors of this volume, were intimately involved in the conception and evolution of World Elder Abuse Awareness Day (WEAAD), helping its founder, Elizabeth Podnieks, to take it from the idea stage (expressed in an informal telephone call early one morning in 2004) to the point where groups and agencies from around the world now routinely organize and host public awareness-raising events on June 15.

In five short years, WEAAD has captured the imagination of people working in the elder abuse and neglect area because they recognized that the topic had to "go public" if a majority of victims were to come forward and seek help, if evidence-based and cost-effective services were to be developed and made available in sufficient quantity to meet current and future needs, and if activities directed at prevention were to be successful. For far too long, elder abuse and neglect has been a hidden problem. As Patricia Brownell points out in Chapter 1, the numbers of older persons are growing in virtually all parts of the world. If current prevalence rates continue to hold, we can expect an increasing number of elder abuse and neglect cases unless steps are taken to address the conditions that lead to its occurrence. She underscores the fact that elder abuse and neglect is not just a developed world phenomenon. Especially worrisome for the future, is the additional fact that the pace of population aging is most rapid in less developed countries that have less infrastructure and fewer resources to offer a burgeoning aging population than the developed world, where the rate of growth was slower. For example, it took France 125 years to reach the point of having 7% of its population aged 65 and over, which defined it as an "old" society, compared with an estimated 25 years to reach this threshold in China. Within the senior population, the most rapid gains in population proportion are among the oldest-old, which is particularly important for estimating the potential size of elder abuse and neglect as a continuing social problem. The oldest-old by definition are the most frail—physically and mentally—so they are the most vulnerable to maltreatment by others.

To date, much of the work on identification, treatment, and prevention of elder abuse and neglect has focused on family dynamics and settings. But population aging is not taking place in a vacuum. Rather, it is occurring simultaneously with other social changes and trends—urbanization and migration are two that seriously impact the older population, leaving many without the safety net of a loving family in geographic proximity to care of them when they are unable to meet their daily needs independently. Falling birth rates mean that in future, many more older people than ever before will have no offspring—loving or unloving, leaving them to be cared for by non-kin or not at all.

There is much discussion in the elder abuse literature about the need for a universally accepted definition of abuse and neglect of older adults that will apply both to situations involving kin and to those involving non-kin, and to both maltreatment that occurs in community settings and that which occurs in institutional settings.

Three definitions are in fairly common use around the world. The first, found on the US National Center on Elder Abuse website, defines it as:

> ... *any knowing, intentional, or negligent act by a caregiver or any other*
> *person that causes harm or a serious risk of harm to a vulnerable adult.*
>
> *NCEA (2008)*

A second definition, used by the US National Research Council's Panel to Review Risk and Prevalence of Elder Abuse and Neglect, places less importance on determining intentionality and draws attention to the relationship between the victim and perpetrator, defining "elder mistreatment" as:

> ... *(a) intentional actions that cause harm or create a serious risk of harm*
> *(whether or not harm is intended) to a vulnerable elder by a caregiver or other*
> *person who stands in a trust relationship to the elder or (b) failure by a care-*
> *giver to satisfy the elder's basic needs or to protect the elder from harm.*
>
> *Bonnie and Wallace (2003, p. 1)*

A third, and perhaps the most commonly used, was developed by the UK's Action on Elder Abuse in 1995 and subsequently adopted by the World Health Organization (WHO) and the International Network for the Prevention of Elder Abuse (INPEA) for their *Missing Voices* project:

> ... *a single or repeated act or lack of appropriate action, occurring within*
> *any relationship where there is an expectation of trust, which causes harm*
> *or distress to an older person.*
>
> *WHO/INPEA (2002, p. 3)*

As Spencer and Gutman (2008) note, the concept of "trust" is a key part of the WHO/INPEA definition. It speaks to an "expectation of trust"—there does not have to be an actual trust relationship between persons. Stones (1995) argues that certain relationships are trust relationships by virtue of kin relationship and social definition (e.g., family, neighbors, friends), or by legal context (contract or specific authority, as in the case of home support workers, health care providers, banking staff, and lawyers).

Spencer and Gutman (2008) note, however, that while the WHO/INPEA definition is useful for some purposes, it tends generally to be imprecise when used as a basis for estimating prevalence, incidence, and risk factors for elder abuse and neglect.

> *At a minimum, a useful definition will be one that can clearly identify scope: who is being harmed (i.e. victims), type of harms, threshold (consequences/ effect) and who is doing the harm (perpetrators).*
> *Spencer and Gutman (2008, p. 10)*

In this volume, several of the authors echo our concern about definitional vagueness. There is also some discussion about the difficulties of estimating the prevalence, incidence, and risk factors for abuse and neglect, due to the use of different research methodologies by different investigators. At the base of this discussion is the fact that this is an extremely complex domain in which, it is generally agreed, an all-hazards or "one-size-fits-all" approach is inappropriate. Lachs and Pillemer (2004) in a now classic article published in *The Lancet* and Garre-Olmo et al. (2009) in a recent article in the *Journal of the American Geriatrics Society* suggest that elder abuse cannot be analyzed as a unitary concept and that risk factors must be assessed for each abuse subtype.

It is our contention that in the development and conduct of research, development of theory and policy, and especially in the practice arena, account must be taken of the diversity of the older population. In Chapter 1, Brownell begins discussion of the topic by citing research that suggests that older adults from different cultures may view abuse differently. She also raises the issue of poverty as a risk factor. In the course of her discussion, she compares and contrasts Canadian and American approaches to intervention, noting that the United States has a more protection-oriented system, while, in Canada, the emphasis is placed on education and prevention.

In Chapter 2, Jill Hightower draws attention to the importance of taking gender into consideration, making the case that the situations of older men and older women who are victims of abuse and neglect are very different—if for no other reason than on account of structural power differences. She argues that the gender-neutral approach of the contemporary elder abuse field misses the key fact that abuse and violence in old age is not gender free nor necessarily age specific but rather, for many, it is part of a continuum of violence across the lifespan. "The 'elder abuse' label actually reflects a societal ageist attitude that homogenizes older people by ignoring differences" within the seniors' population; at the same time, the label magnifies differences between seniors and other age groups. Hightower takes issue with the Violence Against Women movement and the feminist movement for ignoring the plight of older women, who like their younger counterparts may be victims of intimate partner violence. She also takes issue with the tendency of some policymakers and practitioners to base elder abuse counter-measures on the model of child abuse—that is, to consider all older persons as weak, unwilling, or unable to make decisions in their own best interest, and in need of protective services. While this characterization may be true for the most frail, and particular those suffering from moderate to severe dementia, it is certainly not true of the majority.

In Chapter 3, Jordan Kosberg places the spotlight on abused older men, describing them as an invisible and under-studied population. He draws attention to the dangers of sexism, ageism, and stereotyping, using as an example, previously "macho" men who have grown old and who may not be considered as possible victims of abuse. He notes that in inner city and rural locations, and among the homeless, where men predominate numerically, older men may be victimized by younger men (and women). They may also engage in self-neglect to a greater extent than other subpopulations. Yet they are often missed in the planning of mitigation services such as shelters, which are largely targeted to women. Kosberg speaks also of older gay men who may be abused by their partners and/or be victims of systemic abuse and neglect in the social support and health services sectors.

In Chapter 4, Chris Morrissey expands the diversity theme to include lesbian, gay, transgender, and bisexual seniors (LGBT) all of whom may be victims (or perpetrators) of abuse and neglect in intimate partner relationships or in institutional settings. She introduces another "ism" noting that the privileging of heterosexuality over all other sexual orientations is a way of discriminating against and oppressing sexual minorities. Currently, there are an estimated 3 million LGBT seniors in the United States. By 2030, that number is projected to nearly double (National Gay and Lesbian Task Force, 2009). As Morrissey notes, this is a population that traditionally has valued youth and beauty. It must battle ageist attitudes within its own community as well as the heterosexism of those external to it.

Chapter 5 represents a departure from most other books concerned with elder abuse in presenting the perspective of British Columbia's Hospital Employees' Union (HEU), the union that represents the majority of the direct and indirect care staff working in the province's long-term care facilities. Using HEU as an example, Marcy Cohen analyzes the role of unions in abuse prevention at the individual, facility, and system levels. She goes on to suggest that unions have a significant contribution to make to abuse prevention by ensuring due process, encouraging members to report abuse, and developing strategies in coalition with community groups for addressing systemic abuse at the facility and system levels. These strategies include legislation and funding commitments from provincial governments addressing staffing levels and staff training. She bases her arguments on research linking quality of care with working conditions in long-term care facilities.

Chapter 6 is also novel because it presents a criminal justice system perspective viewed through the eyes of a law enforcement officer who works on a daily basis in the elder abuse area. Constable Patricia Fleishmann, using financial abuse as an example, describes a number of gaps in the system, including ageist beliefs held by banking officials, investigating officers, chiefs of police, prosecuting attorneys, and members of the judiciary. These include believing that as a group elderly victims are poor witnesses; that when an elderly victim is the sole witness and he or she is considered cognitively impaired, it is difficult to obtain a conviction without evidence of visible injuries; and that elderly victims are incapable of understanding or handling a criminal prosecution, which is typically a slow and cumbersome process. On the brighter side, Fleishmann describes a number of promising initiatives that have been implemented in the province of Ontario to bridge the gaps. These include the establishment of specialized seniors fraud units, an informal criminal justice organization whose purpose is to facilitate information exchange on a regional basis that may assist with criminal investigations pertaining to financial abuse of older adults by strangers, a comprehensive elder abuse training DVD for police officers, a "Senior Crime Stoppers" telephone tip line, and a "hot line" for at-risk seniors to use to get help in abuse situations.

Chapter 7, the final chapter, describes an innovative inter-generational project that in 2006 brought communication design students and their instructor together with Constable Fleishmann and other experts in elder abuse and resulted in the production of a powerful set of social marketing materials. While no formal follow-up was undertaken, of the impact of these materials on attitudes and behavior of those exposed to them, there were self-reported changes in the students and anecdotal reports from the mentors that suggest change did take place in others. It is our impression that the principles underpinning the project and the procedures it employed are worthy of further consideration. They may prove to be useful tools in combating elder abuse and neglect and the "isms" that sustain it.

There is general agreement that the number of cases reaching the attention of health care providers and the justice system is increasing and that those numbers represent only the tip of the iceberg (O'Keeffe et al., 2007). With the pressures of population aging upon us, it is important to identify and employ any and all measures that will enable communities around the world to move forward and stamp out abuse and neglect of older persons. Especially compelling, and a key theme of this book, is the need to address ageism, which as Brownell notes at the outset, plays an insidious role in setting the stage for abuse and neglect.

References

Bonnie, R.J., Wallace, R.B. (Eds.), 2003. Elder Mistreatment: Abuse, Neglect, and Exploitation in an Aging America. National Academies Press, Washington, DC.

Garre-Olmo, J., Planas-Pujol, X., Lioez-Pousa, S., Juvinya, D., Villa, A., Vilalta-Franch, J., 2009. Prevalence and risk factors of suspected elder abuse subtypes in people aged 75 and older. J. Am. Geriat. Soc. 57, 815–822.

Lachs, M.S., Pillemer, K., 2004. Elder abuse. Lancet 364, 1263–1272.

National Center on Elder Abuse, 2008. What is elder abuse? Retrieved August 20, 2008. <http://www.ncea.aoa.gov/NCEAroot/Main_Site/FAQ/Questions.aspx>

National Gay and Lesbian Task Force, 2009. Challenges facing LGBT elders. Retrieved August 18, 2009. <http://www.thetaskforce.org/issues/aging>

O'Keeffe, M., Hills, A., Doyle, M., McCreadie, C., Scholes, S., Constantine, R., Tinker, A., Manthorpe, J., Biggs, S., Erns, B., 2007. UK Study of Abuse and Neglect of Older People: Prevalence Survey Report. National Centre for Social Research, London.

Spencer, C., Gutman, G., November, 2008. Sharpening Canada's Focus—Developing an Empirical Profile of Abuse and Neglect among Older Women and Men in the Community. Human Resources and Skills Development Canada, Ottawa, ON.

Stones, M., 1995. Scope and definition of elder abuse and neglect in Canada. In: McLean, M.J. (Ed.), Abuse and Neglect of Older Canadians: Strategies for Change. Thompson Educational Publishing, Toronto, ON, pp. 111–115.

WHO/INPEA, 2002. Missing Voices: Views of Older Persons on Elder Abuse. World Health Organization, Geneva.

Contributors' biographies

Patricia Brownell, PhD, LMSW, is Associate Professor of Social Work at the Fordham University Graduate School of Social Service. She is a Hartford Foundation Geriatric Social Work Faculty Scholar, a Ravazzin Center Fellow, and the US Representative to the International Network for the Prevention of Elder Abuse (INPEA). She currently represents INPEA on the United Nations NGO Committee on Ageing in New York and on the Sub-Committee on Older Women (SCOW) of the NGO Committee on the Status of Women (CSW). Dr Brownell is also active in professional organizations at the state and city level. She is immediate past president of the State Society on Aging of New York and in July 2008 became President of the National Association of Social Workers—New York City Chapter. Her areas of research include gerontology, elder abuse, and domestic violence. Dr Brownell has been active in the fields of domestic violence, aging, and public welfare for more than 30 years.

Marcy Cohen, MA, worked since 1996 as the senior researcher and research and policy director for the Hospital Employee's Union of British Columbia. She has co-authored more than 15 research reports and journal articles on implications for staff and patients/residents of long-term care and health restructuring and privatization. Marcy is currently the Chair of the Board for the Canadian Centre for Policy Alternatives BC branch and a past board member of the Vancouver Foundation's Medical Service Foundation and the College of Physicians and Surgeons. She has a long history of working on social justice issues and in community-based research.

Patricia Fleischmann is in her twenty-third year of service with the Toronto Police. She is currently assigned to Community Mobilization with administrative responsibilities for older/vulnerable adult abuse and neglect, as well as mental health issues. She is a graduate of Durham College, McMaster University, and Ryerson University, where she made the Dean's Honour List while receiving her degree in Justice Studies. Her honours thesis was on "Understanding the barriers and challenges that older abused or neglected adults encounter in accessing the Canadian criminal justice system." Presently, she is working toward her Gerontology Certificate at Ryerson University. Constable Fleischmann has worked in all areas of law enforcement, mainly uniform capacity, including primary response and community relations, plus frauds, warrants, and plainclothes duties. She is an active member of the International Association of Women Police, past Special Events Director, currently on the Board of Trustees of Ontario Women in Law Enforcement, and a founding member of Law Enforcement Agencies Protecting Seniors (LEAPS).

Gloria Gutman, PhD, developed and directed the Gerontology Research Centre and Gerontology Department at Simon Fraser University from 1982 to 2005. Currently, she is a co-leader of the BC Network for Aging Research and a Research Associate of the Gerontology Research Centre. She is author/editor of 21 books and more than 150 scholarly articles, chapters, and reports. She served two terms as President of the Canadian Association on Gerontology and was President of the International Association of Gerontology and Geriatrics from 2001 to 2005. She is a Fellow of the Gerontological Society of America and the Canadian Academy of Health Sciences, a member of the World Health Organization's Expert Advisory Panel on Health and Ageing, and a director of the International Institute on Ageing UN-Malta. In 2002, she was appointed as a Special Advisor to the International Network for Prevention of Elder Abuse (INPEA). In 2005, she received the prestigious Rosalie Wolf Memorial Award—International Category from INPEA for her long-term support of elder abuse research and prevention. In 2007, she was awarded the Order of British Columbia for her pioneering work in gerontology research and education.

Jill Hightower, MA, was the Executive Director of the BC Institute Against Family Violence from 1991 until she retired in 1998. Currently, she is a partner with Greta Smith and Henry Hightower in a small research and educational consulting group with a specific focus on social and health issues affecting older adults. Jill has published and presented her research at North American and European conferences and in community forums. In 2006, the group authored a manual on programs and standards for working with older abused women. Jill is the recipient of the Simon Fraser University Gerontology Research Centre Senior Leadership Award. She was a member of the British Columbia Premier's Advisory Council on Aging and Seniors Issues, serves as a member of the Enquiry Committee of the BC College of Psychologists, serves as President of the Sunshine Coast Seniors Network and Advisory Group. Jill continues to advocate personally and professionally for older women.

Jordan I. Kosberg, PhD, ACSW, has been The University of Alabama Endowed Chair of Social Work since 1999. From 1992 to 1995, he was The Philip S. Fisher Professor in the School of Social Work at McGill University. Prof Kosberg has taught at universities in Florida, Ohio, and California, and lectured in Australia, China, Hong Kong, Israel, and New Zealand. He is a Fellow of the Gerontological Society of America, editor/co-editor of eight books, author/co-author of 25 book chapters, and more than 100 journal articles. He is a former member of the Board of Directors of the International Network for the Prevention of Elder Abuse and served on the US National Institute on Aging Developmental Research of Elder Mistreatment's Peer Review Panel. He is a member of the Men's Health Network Board of Advisors and a member of the Editorial Board for the *Journal of Elder Abuse and Neglect*.

Chris Morrissey, BA, is employed at The Centre, a community centre in Vancouver, BC serving and supporting lesbian, gay, transgender, bisexual (LGTB) people and their allies. For the past seven years, she has been the coordinator of the LGTB Generations Project, which serves aging and older LGTB people and brings generations together. She has developed programs for aging and older LGTB people and is involved in education of health care and social services providers and students. Together with a working group of service providers in the seniors services sector, she developed a tool kit to assist agencies with organizational change to provide culturally relevant services for LGTB elders. She is an advocate for LGTB older adults and believes that a lack of culturally relevant services is systemic neglect and abuse. In 2008, she was honored with the Simon Fraser University Gerontology Research Centre Senior Leadership Award. For more than 25 years, she has been an educator of people from elementary school to adulthood. She has worked in Canada, the United States, Malaysia, Brunei, and Chile.

Paul Shecter, MFA, RGD, is Professor of Visual Communication Design at Seneca College in Toronto and a member of the Association of Registered Graphic Designers of Ontario. As preparation for his second career, in teaching, he completed a Master of Fine Arts at York University in 1998. Before that, although he specialized in typographic design, he had worked in a wide variety of capacities in communication design for 28 years. Thus, his experience includes a wealth of real-world scenarios to draw on when he is creating curriculum for his students.

Charmaine Spencer, LLM, is a lawyer and researcher with the Gerontology Research Centre at Simon Fraser University. She is a founding member of the Canadian Network for Prevention of Elder Abuse (CNPEA), taking on many roles, including webmaster and co-editor of the *CNPEA Newsletter*. Since 2007, she has served as co-chair of the Board of Directors. In 2006, she co-created the federal-provincial-territorial materials prepared for the inauguration of World Elder Abuse Awareness Day in Canada. For the past four years, she has been INPEA's representative for Canada. Her research has included many Canadian firsts in building knowledge in the area of abuse in later life, including mental health aspects and social costs. She has developed discussion documents for the federal government and provincial groups on various aspects of abuse and neglect in later life, as well as on seniors at risk, and on substance use/mental health in later life.

1 Social issues and social policy response to abuse and neglect of older adults

Patricia Brownell

This chapter addresses four main issues: (1) Social issues related to abuse and neglect of older adults; (2) challenges in social policy response to abuse and neglect of older adults; (3) US public policy responses to senior abuse at the national and state levels; and (4) international public policy promotion.

Social issues related to abuse and neglect of older adults

Ageism and lack of respect

Ageism is defined as the denial of basic human rights of older persons and is considered one of the most pervasive prejudices across human society, in spite of professed worship and valuing of older adults in many societies, according to the International Longevity Center (ILC) in its publication *Ageism in America* (International Longevity Center, 2006). While combating ageism is of paramount importance in ensuring the human rights of older adults, Dr Robert Butler—who coined the word *ageism* in 1968—notes that it still thrives in cultures and societies.

Ageism is reflected in workplace discrimination, health care discrimination, and discrimination in nursing homes—evidenced by lack of adequate staff, in the media, and in emergency services. It is also reflected in senior abuse. In the United States, it is estimated that 1–3 million adults age 65 and over have been injured, exploited, or otherwise mistreated by someone on whom they depend for care, protection, and love. The ILC report identifies two categories of ageism. The first creates and perpetuates ageism: social forces that shape attitudes about aging, and the media and marketing strategies that present negative depictions of older adults and the aging process. The second is what could be termed personal and institutional ageism: the tendency to dismiss signs of pathological and treatable signs of aging and "normal aging" in medical practices and nursing home facilities, the devaluing of older workers, and the lack of sufficient attention to cruelty toward older adults, resulting in low reporting and lack of attention by policymakers.

Social biases that privilege frailty and protection over empowerment of older adults

The legal principle of *parens patriae*, from English Common Law, underlies much of public policy legislated to protect children. Sadly, it is too often used as a guiding principle for senior abuse protection as well (Kapp, 1999). One aging service agency in New York, which was participating in an empowerment-oriented intervention for older adult victims of family mistreatment, was told by its government funding source that it could not be considered as a reimbursable service because it was not "therapeutic." This intervention, which trained older women who experienced family abuse in the skills necessary to become peer support counselors, public speakers about senior abuse in their communities, and legislative advocates, was designed as a feminist intervention to move older women from perceiving themselves as victims to experiencing themselves as survivors. However, it challenged the legislative intent of public funding appropriations and was considered to be noncompliant with regulatory mandates. Guardianship laws can protect older adults who lack capacity from exploitation and harm; according to Quinn (2004), however, they also strip older adults of civil rights and can make them more vulnerable to exploitation by an unscrupulous and even a well-meaning guardian.

Difficulties current generation of older adults experience in speaking out against their own experience of abuse

The preceding example shows the importance of senior abuse victims and advocates speaking out against abuse and demanding laws, programs, and funding that support older adults to take charge of their own lives and the policies that these reflect. In considering some of the important social movements in the United States, such as the civil rights movement, the women's movement, the domestic violence, gay rights, disabilities and even the "age movement" of the 1950s, 1960s, and 1970s (Blau and Abramovitz, 2003), one of the key elements of success was the victims' willingness to speak out frankly to the media and in public forums. Older people experiencing family mistreatment have traditionally had a harder time speaking out against the mistreatment they experienced and the need for public policy remedies. Support for older adults who are willing to do so may move forward the senior abuse movement by exposing to public scrutiny the ageism underlying their own situations and those in their cohort.

Aging of the population: a global phenomenon in developed countries and countries under development

We have all heard a lot about the baby boomers, those in the United States and Canada born between 1946 and 1964. According to Joanna Mellor and Helen Rehr in their edited book *Can My Eighties Be Like My Fifties?* (Mellor and Rehr, 2005), in 2011, the number of baby boomers in the United States will exceed twice the total population of Canada. According to them, by the second half of the century, the older American population of 84.5 million will be dwarfed by the projected 331 million older people in China who, they say, will nearly equal the total projected population of all ages in the United States. Canada is graying as well. While smaller than the United States (33.8 million people, compared with the US's 283 million), in 2000, people 60+ represented a slightly larger proportion of its population (16.7% compared with 16.5% in the US). By 2050, Canada is expected to have 30.5% of its population 60+, compared with the United States at 26.9%, according to the United Nations Department of Economic and Social Affairs (2002).

WORLD POPULATION AGING: PERCENT OF POPULATION AGE 60+

	2000	2050
World	10.0% of 6.1B	21.1% of 9.3B
Canada	16.7% of 30.8M	30.5% of 40.4M
USA	16.5% of 283.2M	26.9% of 397.0M
Italy	24.1% of 57.5M	42.3% of 43.0M
Cameroon	5.6% of 14.9M	11.2% of 32.3M

World population is projected to increase 50% from 2000 to 2050, from 6.1 billion to 9.3 billion.
World population aging in this period:
• Median age in 2000: 26.5
• Median age in 2050: 36.2
Source: United Nations Department of Economic and Social Affairs (2002).

As more people live longer, some studies estimate that an increasing proportion of the older population will experience debilitating disorders, such as Alzheimer's disease, and be more vulnerable to family and institutional abuse and mistreatment. The fact remains that most older adults live independent and productive lives into advanced old age. However, if current senior abuse prevalence data continue to hold, larger numbers of older people can mean increased cases of senior abuse unless vigorous efforts are mounted to address ageism in all its forms and prevent senior abuse through education, policies, and programs that have been empirically tested as effective.

Diversity of older adults (ethnic, cultural, mental, cognitive, and physical)

The *New York Times* recently reported that for the first time in its history, the New York metropolitan area included more people of color than Caucasians. Both the United States and Canada share a rich history of immigration and a troubled history of Native Americans or First Nation people who have suffered oppression and persecution in the hands of white settlers. We can celebrate the diversity of our respective national heritages as we recognize the inequality of circumstances that people bring with them as they age.

The 2002 United States Census report for New York City (New York City Department for the Aging, 2000) found that the majority of the oldest-old tended to be Caucasian, while the young-old (those moving into their 1960s and 1970s), were increasingly people of color and people who were foreign born. This has important implications for policymaking and service delivery and makes it even more imperative that the voices are heard of all older adults, including the "missing voices" heard in the qualitative study on elder abuse from a global perspective that the International Network for Prevention of Elder Abuse (INPEA) collaborated on with the World Health Organization (WHO/INPEA, 2002). Studies on senior abuse and diversity, such as one conducted by Moon (1998) with Korean older adults, or Brown (1998) with American Indian elders, suggest that older adults from diverse cultures view senior abuse differently, and these diverse perspectives need to be heard and accounted for in policy advocacy efforts.

Differences in life situations of older women and older men

Chapter 2 discusses gender difference in senior abuse in some detail, so I will not take up a lot of time on this. We know that older women move into old age less advantaged financially than older men, and single women of color are the least advantaged. In the United States, the most economically disadvantaged cohort of older people are Latino older women who are single and living among or with non-family household members. Gender biases in the family have historically made women more vulnerable to domestic violence, and many studies have suggested that this continues into old age, with adult sons as well as older spouses and partners abusing older women (Hightower and Hightower, 2004). In Chapter 4, Jordan Kosberg discusses the vulnerability of older men.

Families in later life

When the first White House Conference on Aging was held in 1961 in the United States, the poverty measure was being invented by Mollie Orshansky, a home economist with the federal social security department (Fisher, 1992). At that time, older adults were shown in the aggregate to be the poorest of all age groups in the country. With changes in social security law and pensions, now older people are relatively advantaged (the poverty rate for older adults is about 10%, compared with almost twice that for children). While this is a great advance and demonstrates the success of social welfare policy targeted to older adults in the United States, it has sometimes resulted in seniors being exploited by younger family members who cannot afford to own their own homes and maintain a steady income, whether through unemployment, substance abuse, or mental illness. Many older people would rather care for their impaired family members than see them out on the street, but this can put them at great risk. According to one prosecutor in Brooklyn, all the elder abuse homicides in the first half of 2001 in Brooklyn were perpetrated by mentally ill adult sons against older parents who took them in when psychiatric institutions, jails, and prisons failed in doing adequate discharge planning (Arlene Markarian, Assistant District Attorney, Brooklyn District Attorney's Office, October 10, 2004, personal communication). This suggests that a holistic approach to senior abuse prevention must include institutions and professionals not commonly associated with aging service provision.

Differences and similarities in community and institutional senior abuse

We tend to dichotomize community and institutional abuse perhaps more than is necessary. With community abuse, we are concerned with the right to autonomy and decision making for the older adults who experience senior abuse. In nursing homes, the care dependency needs of older residents may supersede their right to self-determination as well. In the United States, we have a nursing home ombudsman program where volunteers who serve as advocates for residents and their families are empowered to speak for the resident or family member when facility mistreatment is noted. Operated through our aging service network, it has the potential to mitigate against abuse and mistreatment of residents by serving as the voice of residents who may feel or actually be powerless to protest poor treatment on their own (Menio and Keller, 2000). More research is needed to assess the effectiveness of this program in preventing senior abuse in institutional settings.

Complex social responses to diverse forms of senior abuse

What we identify as senior abuse takes many forms, and senior victims of abuse are themselves diverse in terms of capacity, care dependency needs, and access to family supports and resources. This in itself is a social issue that moves us to the next topic I was asked to address: challenges for social policy responses to senior abuse. If policymakers in Canada are like those in the United States, they prefer clear, simple, and easily understood policy issues to address in the policymaking process. Senior abuse as we know it is anything but simple!

Social policy response to abuse and neglect of older adults: challenges

Prevention and early intervention versus protection

Prevention and early intervention as service concepts come from public health and have been applied to senior abuse (Rapp-Paglicci and Dulmus, 2005). Early efforts to address senior abuse in the United States focused on detection and crisis intervention. Prevention and early intervention models began to emerge fairly recently and reflect the increasingly multidisciplinary approach to senior abuse and the emergence of research that examines risk factors and service outcomes. Some research has suggested that older adult victims of abuse are not different in any significant way from other older people in their cohort, and that the risk factors, such as substance abuse, mental illness, dementia, and past history of violence or criminality, are on the abuser side. Researchers such as Podnieks (1992) and others have identified some evidence that older women who have had histories of victimization, including child abuse or poor past relationships with caregivers (Reis, 2000), may be at risk of reestablishing abusive relationships at later stages in their lives.

Some examples of prevention include coalitions and consortiums with communication, collaboration, and education as a primary objective. Some health professionals such as nurses and dentists have adopted universal health screening procedures through association sponsorship. Bar associations educate members on financial abuse of older adults. Early education in primary and secondary schools represent an early intervention model. In New York City, Civil Court Judge Fern Fisher initiated with the local government aging agency an assigned counsel program pairing social workers and attorneys to work with older adults coming to housing court with evictions (Nanos, 2006). A significant number were found to be victims of financial exploitation by family members and even friends and strangers who they invited into their homes to share their increasing rent and were instead robbed and left unable to keep up with their payments. In extreme cases of elder abuse, forensic detection centers have been developed in California, as interdisciplinary centers, some attached to universities, which include physicians, lawyers, nurses, social workers, and forensic psychologists (Wiglesworth et al., 2006).

Overall, the United States has evolved a more protection-oriented service system than Canada. In the 1970s, with federalizing of old-age assistance (Title One of the Social Security Act) and the deinstitutionalization movement, states created an adult protective service system, operated by either the counties or the states directly. The underlying assumptions of these programs were that clients would be primarily self-neglecting or a danger to themselves or others and would be served as single-case entities. In the 1980s and 1990s, a number of states passed elder abuse mandatory reporting laws that were overlaid on the county Adult Protective Services (APS) programs. Concerns about under-funding of services to support these programs, as well as concerns about ageism and overriding the decision making of older adults slowed the process of these laws. However, currently all but six states operate under mandated reporting of elder abuse in the community, and all states have some form of mandatory reporting law for institutional abuse. New York is one of the states without a mandatory reporting law for community-dwelling older adult residents because of concerns about civil liberties of older adults, and it is much more like Canada than most other states in its approach to elder abuse and its emphasis on education and prevention, as opposed to protection.

Social health and service versus criminal justice response

Early research on elder abuse suggested that it stemmed from caregiver stress, and adult daughters were the most likely perpetrators of older women victims. This view of causation prompted many practitioners to advocate for social service responses to senior abuse. Later research, by Karl Pillemer (Pillemer and Finkelhor, 1989) and others, found that adult child abusers were often substance abusers and committed criminal acts against their parents. Domestic violence (DV) advocates noted cases of senior abuse that appeared much like traditional DV case situations with older men continuing to abuse older women after a lifetime of abuse and advocated for a criminal justice response. A study of two programs—one that focused primarily on a family service approach to abuse and the other on a criminal justice approach—found that both relied heavily on social services to supplement any criminal justice (meaning court or law enforcement actions) to be effective (Brownell and Wolden, 2002).

Geriatric versus feminist perspective

Early studies in the field of elder abuse identified frail, care-dependent older adults as those most at risk of experiencing abuse by family caregivers, most frequently adult daughter caregivers. Self-neglect is the most frequently cited form of elder mistreatment identified through county and state APS programs in the United States (Dyer and Goins, 2000). In contrast, some elder abuse experts point to patterns of familial abuse that reflect dynamics of power and control, similar to those seen in abuse of younger female victims by spouses and partners (Brandl, 2000). Recent studies on senior abuse challenge the view that mistreatment of older adults is caused by caregiver stress, and instead suggest that the traditional domestic violence framework explains mistreatment of older adults more effectively (Pillemer and Finkelhor, 1989; Vinton, 1999).

Lack of clear and consistent definitions and reliable and quantifiable data

It is a commonly cited concern among senior abuse advocates and policymakers that programs serving mistreated older adults suffer from unclear definitions, a weak research base, undeveloped causal theories, and untested practice models (St James, 2001). The Elder Justice Act, pending in the US Congress, represents an effort to address these concerns on a national level by providing a uniform statutory definition of senior abuse, and funding for prevalence research and program evaluation. The Madrid 2002 International Plan of Action on Ageing (MIPAA), which emerged from the Second World Assembly on Ageing held in Madrid in April 2002, also laid out a set of definitions for older adult abuse and a plan of action for participating nations to implement. To date, however, we have almost no good outcome research on elder abuse laws, programs, and policies in the United States, which is one of the issues that the Elder Justice Act could address if passed. In terms of implementing MIPAA, this is something with which each government has to struggle, in collaboration with partnering non-governmental organizations (NGOs) (especially academic institutions). Questions that could be posed include: What are reliable and valid outcome measures? What are good and bad laws?

Lack of perceived power among victims and providers to effect change in public policy

This is certainly an issue among older women and men in the United States. In early 2006, I initiated an intervention in collaboration with a not-for-profit agency in New York City to train older women who had experienced family mistreatment to become peer counselors, public speakers, and legislative advocates using the NOVA House elder abuse training manual. Of 14 women who participated in the training, two elected to get further legislative advocacy training through the J-PAC senior leadership program sponsored by the Jewish Association of Services for the Aged, and three spoke out about their abusive relationships at an elder abuse conference held at Fordham University in June 2006. This is a very small sample, from a research or public policy perspective, but it is a start.

Lack of consensus among provider and advocacy community on remedies

In the United States, APS laws generally stipulate the least intrusive intervention, but what does that mean when a capacitated older adult chooses to remain in an extremely degrading and exploitative relationship? An example from the newspapers is the story of two elderly sisters who took in a substance-abusing nephew, who took all their money and then sent them out to beg in the street so he could get more money for his drug habit (Kleinfield, 2004). A number of agencies were involved to no avail. Finally, a woman police detective got one of the sisters to tell her story and then had the nephew arrested. With the sisters intervening, the judge mandated him into residential treatment. He came out, moved back in with the sisters, and the cycle started all over again. The next time he was jailed, and then placed in a halfway house. The sisters and he still want to have contact with each other.

In other cases, an older person who meets nursing home criteria can—hypothetically—be placed in a nursing home against his or her will (generally through a guardianship proceeding), and one study suggested that this can hasten their death (Lachs, 1998). Is it because they are very ill at that point, or because they were removed from familiar—if abusive and unsafe—surroundings, and placed in an unfamiliar setting? Beneficence versus autonomy is at the heart of what social workers struggle with and why social workers shudder when prosecutors say "Treat them like homicides!" meaning get the abusive perpetrator loved one sentenced and keep the older adult victim from talking in court. Among professionals and older adults, there may be a difference in opinion about remedies. Older people may want their abusive loved one to get help, social workers may want the older person to voluntarily renounce the abusive relationship, and prosecutors may want to punish the abuser.

Fragmentation, service gaps, lack of funding, and under-funding for services to older adults and their families

In APS, federal funding comes from the Social Service Block Grant, which is capped and used for many other needed services such as DV, day care, and senior centers. The APS proportion in New York State amounts to 2% (Susan B. Somers, Associate Commissioner, New York State Office of Children and Family Services, May 6, 2006, personal communication). The balance must be made up with city and state tax levy and always falls short of the need. Even in service-rich systems such as New York City, the local department of social services (including APS), the aging service network, and the DV service network have a difficult time communicating, and this is among the public agencies alone (Brownell et al., 2005).

United States public policy responses

Two legislative examples

Elder abuse has been primarily identified as a state social welfare issue by the US federal government. Two exceptions include the Older Americans Act (OAA), legislated in 1965, and the Violence Against Women Act (VAWA), legislated in 1994. Elder abuse was addressed in amendments to these acts in 1992 (OAA) and 2000 (VAWA).

Older Americans Act of 1965

The Older Americans Act was legislated after the first White House Conference on Aging (1961) and created a network of services to older adults that was intended to promote their independence and ability to live independently in the community for as long as possible. It created a Federal Administration on Aging headed by an Assistant Secretary in the (now) US Department of Health and Human Services that promoted social inclusion for older adults.

The 1992 Amendment to Older Americans Act: Title VII (Elder Rights and Resources) established elder abuse counseling and related services; health insurance counseling; legal assistance; the Long Term Care Ombudsman Program; and state and local programs to prevent fraud and abuse.

Violence Against Women Act (1994)

The Violence Against Women Act was passed in 1994 as part of an omnibus crime control act. It created an Office on Violence Against Women in the

US Department of Justice. The Violence Against Women Act (VAWA): 2000 and 2006 Amendments established safe homes for older women; law enforcement and cross training to address older women victims of domestic and sexual violence; multidisciplinary collaborative community responses to senior abuse victims; and culturally and linguistically relevant services. The amendments also mandated that priority be given to the needs of the underserved.

Example of a US national coalition building effort

A National Elder Abuse Summit was held in Washington, DC in December 2001. A *Blueprint for Action* emerged from the Summit that established 10 priorities. First among them was to support a National Elder Abuse Act. A National Elder Justice Coalition was formed to support the promulgation of this act, and with Senate co-sponsors John Breaux and Orin Hatch, advocated for the Elder Justice Act. This bill, which is still pending in Congress, would create an Office of Elder Justice in the US Department of Health and Human Services. Currently, the Elder Justice Act has not yet been passed into federal law, but supporters of the bill are hopeful that it will pass into law within the next few legislative sessions.

Example of a state/local coalition building effort

Project 2015, published in 2000, is a collaborative project between the New York State Office of the Aging (SOFA) and the State Society on Aging (SSA) of New York. It had its genesis in 1998, with the shared concern of SOFA and SSA that the baby boomers would begin entering old age in 2015 in New York State, and there had been no efforts on the part of state or local governments to anticipate the issues that might arise at this future time (Dr Joanna Mellor, Past President, State Society on Aging of New York, May 7, 2006, personal communication).

SOFA and SSA decided to collaborate on a series of papers on 24 key topics related to the aging of the baby boomers, including long-term care, transportation, and elder abuse. Experts in academia and agency-based practice were invited to contribute papers on these topics, which were compiled and printed in a briefing book by SOFA. The New York State governor at that time (Governor George Pataki) then asked each of his state commissioners to respond to the articles by drafting a plan for how each gubernatorial agency would be ready to respond to the stated issues by 2015. This resulted in a publication of a white paper (Pataki and Pine, 2002), which became a roadmap for state government to use in anticipating the impact of the aging of the New York State population.

This collaboration between academics and state government officials was perceived to lend legitimacy to the policymaking process, first at the executive government branch level and later at the legislative level. The SSA of New York, in collaboration with the SOFA, identified one topic from *Project 2015* as the focus for its legislative town hall meeting at its annual conference. This resulted in an opportunity for ongoing dialogue among academics, practitioners, government officials, and legislators providing increased access and opportunity to advocate for policy changes and exchange of ideas and information.

Six years ago, the governor's office with some non-profit agencies hosted an elder abuse summit, which used the article on elder abuse from *Project 2015* as the framework for beginning the dialogue (Caccamise and Mason, 2004). During the 2005 White House Conference on Aging, held once every 10 years, the New York Governor's Office and the New York SOFA and state delegates strategized effectively to vote a resolution on elder abuse #15 in a list of 73 resolutions, giving this national prominence (Susan B. Somers, Assistant Commissioner for Adult Protective Services, New York State Office of Children and Families, May 7, 2006, personal communication). Three important US public policies, Older Americans Act Reauthorization (title 7), the Elder Justice Act (still a bill), and the 2006 amendment to the Violence Against Women Act (VAWA III), all address elder mistreatment at the national level, and all were the result of local and state coalitions advocating for public policy change at the national level. The Madrid 2002 International Plan of Action on Ageing (elder abuse and mistreatment) represents a similar effort at the international level.

International public policy to address senior abuse

The Madrid 2002 International Plan of Action on Ageing establishes objectives and action steps to promote public policies and programs in nations around the world. Priority direction III: Ensuring enabling and supportive environments—Issue 3: Neglect, abuse, and violence includes the following objectives:

Objective One: Elimination of all forms of neglect, abuse, and violence of older persons.
Objective Two: Creation of support services to address elder abuse. (Brownell, 2003).
   The Plan can be found at http://www.un.org/esa/socdev/ageing/mipaa.html (retrieved from Internet on July 22, 2008).

Currently the United Nations is monitoring the implementation of the MIPAA, in a process called Madrid Plus Five (or, five years after the promulgation of the plan of action in 2002). This is a grassroots "bottom-up" review, with the assumption of the availability of "top-down" support. Governments can decide what part(s) of MIPAA to monitor; however, NGOs must advocate with governments on what part(s) of MIPAA to include in the monitoring plan. But first, NGOs and older adults must advocate with governments to participate in the review; and secondly, they must advocate for governments to include the elder abuse objectives as part of their review. The United Nations Secretary General supports and provides technical assistance through two offices: the Department of Economic and Social Affairs (DESA), and the Department of Public Information (DPI).

The General Assembly (representing governments) oversaw the hearings on Madrid Plus Five through the Commission on Social Development (CSD), which will oversee the Madrid Plus5 monitoring plan and implementation, based on the following timetable:

2006: Nations that signed onto MIPAA identified what sections they planned to include in their monitoring plan. This provided opportunities for Canadian senior abuse advocates to have input into the Canadian plan.

February 2007: At CSD, member nations reported on laws passed, programs established, and services initiated since the implementation of MIPAA (without outcome analyses), and on what aspects of MIPAA they had decided to review.

During 2007, a "bottom-up" action review appraisal took place on those aspects of MIPAA selected for monitoring (review).

February 2008: At CSD, governments presented their responses to what they had found about the following:
- Impact of policies, programs, and other initiatives
- Outcomes for older adults
- Direction of future social welfare policies

There has been an important role throughout this process for elder abuse advocates, NGOs, and academic institutions in determining what constitutes "good" and "bad" laws; how older persons' rights are balanced against intrusive "protection"; and what good a law is without adequate funding to implement it.

In 2006, the United Nations promulgated guidelines for the review and appraisal of MIPAA (United Nations Department of Economic and Social Affairs, 2006), and these were distributed to the member nations. CSD approved the modality for the first review and appraisal and endorsed the calendar to start the global review in 2007 and report back in 2008. CSD also established the theme for the first review at the global level, "Addressing the Challenges and Opportunities of Ageing," and provided the venue of the review in 2007 and 2008, plenary debates, a series of panel discussions, and events.

Major findings from the reviews and appraisals demonstrated that progress has been made in all regions in implementing provisions of the MIPAA. The implementation has been uneven, however, according to the Chairman's summary of the panel discussion of the regional review and appraisal of the MIPAA held at the 40th Session of the Commission on Social Development (United Nations Commission on Social Development, 2008).

Positive findings include that the issue of poverty for older adults has been put on the agenda across all regions, and many countries are examining ways to extend social protection to all workers and introduce universal social protection on the agenda. There is evidence of an increase at the national level in developing institutional mechanisms for creating focal points on aging, as well as specific policies, action plans, and programs on aging. Additional training in geriatrics for medical staff has been initiated, and supports have been created for promoting "aging in place" (United Nations Commission on Social Development, 2008).

Continued challenges include the need to promote awareness about linking aging and development, creating an age disaggregated database, adjusting and increasing the level of social services for home care and supports for family caregivers, and managing an aging workforce. Access to high-quality and affordable health care remains a challenge for all the regions of the world. Future priorities that were identified in the review process include continuing promotion of lifelong, healthy aging; increasing participation of older adults in all aspects of social and civic life; and promoting age-friendly physical environments (United Nations Commission on Social Development, 2008).

The World Health Organization (WHO), the NGO Committee on Ageing, and INPEA are taking the lead in promoting global awareness of elder abuse through educational programs and the World Elder Abuse Awareness Day project, which has been held on June 15 every year since 2006. The NGO Committee on Ageing, which is an umbrella organization for more than 45 NGOs with an aging focus, supports education and awareness about senior abuse. For example, during the past three years, it sponsored two programs on elder abuse at the United Nations in New York City. Speakers included Jill and Dr Henry Hightower, who spoke on issues related to older women victims of family mistreatment in March 2006, Dr Jordan Kosberg, who spoke about issues related to the abuse of older men in April 2006, and Dr Ariela Lowenstein, who presented on elder abuse in Israel in June 2007.

INPEA has undertaken an Environmental Scan on elder abuse, which provides critical information on elder abuse from a global perspective, to complement government reports on MIPAA social policy responses to senior abuse. In May 2008, with input from INPEA, the UN Department of Public Affairs held a briefing on elder abuse as an important issue of international concern. The briefing, *Be a Better Neighbor: Prevent Elder Abuse*, included a panel that explored the many ways that elder abuse occurs in the world and the importance of developing new preventive strategies to combat this social problem (United Nations Department of Public Information, 2008).

Conclusion

The United States and Canada are different in their social policy response to senior abuse. However, there are many ways that we can collaborate with each other to promote greater awareness about the need for public policy, services, and funding to support greater awareness about senior abuse and how to prevent it. Examples include sharing information on public policies and coalition building at conferences; collaborating on responses to the Madrid Plus Five monitoring and review process; contributing to journals and publications such as the *Journal of Elder Abuse and Neglect* and the *Journal of Gerontological Social Work*; and sharing other ideas. (Let's keep talking!)

References

Blau, J., Abramovitz, M., 2003. The Dynamics of Social Welfare Policy. Oxford University Press, New York, NY.

Brandl, B., 2000. Power and control: understanding domestic abuse in later life. Generations 24 (11), 39–45.

Brown, A., 1998. Patterns of abuse among Native American elderly. In: Tatara, T. (Ed.), Understanding Elder Abuse in Minority Populations. Brunner/Mazel, Philadelphia, PA, pp. 143–159.

Brownell, P., 2003. Madrid 2002: global ageing and violence against older persons post 9/11. New Glob. Dev. 19 (1), 15–25.

Brownell, P., Wolden, A., 2002. Elder abuse intervention strategies: social service or criminal justice? J. Gerontol. Soc. Work 40 (1/2), 83–100.

Brownell, P., Berman, J., Jennings, P., 2005. Unfunded Grant Application Submitted to the National Institute of Justice. Fordham University, New York, NY.

Caccamise, P.L., Mason, A., 2004. Policy paper: New York State Summit Targets Elder Abuse, "The time to act is now." J. Elder Abuse Negl. 16 (4), 41–61.

Dyer, C.B., Goins, A.M., 2000. The role of the interdisciplinary geriatric assessment in addressing self-neglect of the elderly. Generations 24 (11), 23–27.

Fisher, G.M., 1992. The development and history of the poverty thresholds. Soc. Secur. Bull. 55 (4), 3–14. <http://www.aspe.hhs.gov/poverty/papers/hptgssiv.htm>

Hightower, J., Hightower, H., 2004. Age, gender and violence: abuse against older women. Geriatr. Aging 7 (3), 60–63.

International Longevity Center, 2006. Ageism in America. ILC, New York, NY.

Kapp, M.B., 1999. Geriatrics and the Law. Springer Publishing Company, New York, NY.

Kleinfield, N.R., December 12, 2004. Bowed by age and battered by an addicted nephew. N.Y. Times. <Retrieved from Internet on April 10, 2006: http://www.nytimes.com/2004/12/12/nyregion/12elder.html?ei=5090&en=37b2d4704da6f217&ex>

Lachs, M.S., 1998. The mortality of elder abuse. JAMA 280 (5), 428–432.

Mellor, M.J., Rehr, H. (Eds.), 2005. Baby Boomers: Can My Eighties Be Like My Fifties? Springer Publishing Company, New York, NY, pp. 1–7.

Menio, D., Keller, B.H., 2000. CARIE: a multifaceted approach to abuse prevention in nursing homes. Generations 24 (11), 28–38.

Moon, A., 1998. Elder abuse and neglect among Korean elderly in the United States. In: Tatara, T. (Ed.), Understanding Elder Abuse in Minority Populations. Brunner/Mazel, Philadelphia, PA, pp. 109–118.

Nanos, J., February 12, 2006. Agencies join forces to aid older tenants. N.Y. Times B44.

New York City Department for the Aging, 2000. Census Data for New York City Residents Aged 60+. Office of the Mayor, New York, NY.

Pataki, G.E., Pine, P.P., 2002. Project 2015—State agencies prepare for the impact of an aging New York. White paper for discussion. New York State Office for the Aging, Albany, NY.

Pillemer, K., Finkelhor, D., 1989. Causes of elder abuse: caregiver stress versus problem relatives. Am. J. Orthopsychiatry 59 (2), 51–57.

Podnieks, E., 1992. National survey on abuse of the elderly in Canada. J. Elder Abuse Negl. 4 (1/2), 5–58.

Quinn, M.J., 2004. Guardianships of Adults: Achieving Justice, Autonomy, and Safety. Springer Publishing Company, New York, NY.

Rapp-Paglicci, L.A., Dulmus, C.N., 2005. Prevention across the adult life span. In: Dulmus, C.N., Rapp-Paglicci, L.A. (Eds.), Handbook of Preventions for Adults. John Wiley & Sons, Hoboken, NJ, pp. 3–9.

Reis, M., 2000. The IOA Screen: an abuse-alert measure that dispels myths. Generations 24 (11), 13–16.

St James, P., 2001. Challenges in elder mismanagement programs and policy. J. Gerontol. Soc. Work 36 (3/4), 127–140.

United Nations Commission on Social Development, 2008. Chairman's Summary— Panel discussion: Regional review and appraisal of the Madrid International Plan of Action on Ageing, 8 February 2008. <Retrieved on August 1, 2008, from http://www.un.org/esa/socdev/csd/csocd2008/Documents/summary2.pdf>

United Nations Department of Economic and Social Affairs, 2002. World Population Ageing 1950–2050. UN/DESA, Population Division, New York, NY.

United Nations Department of Economic and Social Affairs, 2006. Guidelines for Review and Appraisal of the Madrid International Plan of Action on Ageing: Bottom-up Participatory Approach. UN/DESA, New York, NY.

United Nations Department of Public Information, 2008. Be a Better Neighbor: Prevent Elder Abuse: summary. <Retrieved on August 1, 2008, from http://www.un.org/dpi/ngosection/index.asp#>

Vinton, L., 1999. Working with abused older women from a feminist perspective. J. Women Aging 11 (2/3), 85–100.

WHO/INPEA, 2002. Missing Voices: Views of Older Persons on Elder Abuse. World Health Organization, Geneva. <http://www.who.int/ageing/projects/elder_abuse/missing_voices/en/index.html>

Wiglesworth, A., Mosqueda, L., Burnight, K., Younglove, T., Jeske, D., 2006. Findings from an elder abuse forensic center. Gerontologist 46 (2), 277–283.

2 Abuse in later life: when and how does gender matter?

Jill Hightower

If we are to fully address issues of violence and abuse in the lives of older adults across all nation states, we must move beyond the current narrow, gender-neutral focus of the field of elder abuse. We must recognize that abuse and violence in old age is neither gender free nor necessarily related to the age of the victim but part of a continuum of violence across the lifespan. The "elder abuse" label actually reflects a societal predisposition to homogenize older people by ignoring differences among them, including gender. Assuming that gender does not matter is both a poor basis for research and a bad basis for public policy. This chapter examines the role and the relationship between gender and age in abuse in later life from the perspective of an older adult who has worked on issues of family violence during her professional career.

Gender refers to socially constructed differences between sexes, and to the social relationships between women and men. These differ across cultures and change over time. Women's and men's responsibilities and roles in society are socially determined. How we are perceived and how we are expected to think and act as women or men is a function of gender, not because of biological differences but because of cultural norms in society. Gender influences access to resources and opportunities and shapes life choices at every stage through life. These gendered experiences impact on the health and well-being of both women and men in later years. In today's world, we are witness to the gradual change over time in western society in gender roles and responsibilities. In some other countries and cultures, gender roles are most often prescribed by traditional cultural norms. However, gender is a significant factor in relation to abuse in later life (as in earlier life), regardless of culture or societal norms.

Some older women and men experience abuse. But violence and abuse are facts of life for many women of all ages. Living with abuse by a loved one has serious negative consequences for their quality of life. When age alone becomes the focus and central defining element of an issue of abuse and neglect in later life, the realities of lives of many older women are ignored (Hightower et al., 2001). These women are trapped between two perceived social and health problems: violence against women (domestic violence) and elder abuse. The result is that abused older women's needs are more often than not overlooked.

Alcalde (2005) argues that although violence and abuse happen across the lifespan, researchers, practitioners, and policymakers have created silos: child abuse, woman abuse, and elder abuse. In this process, not only have we worked separately from our colleagues in other areas but also, she suggests, we have put people into "boxes" so that as an older adult they may either experience elder abuse or domestic violence, not both.

Defining elder abuse and violence against women

In the Violence Against Women field, violence and abuse in the lives of women is viewed as a human rights issue involving both gender and power/control. In the Elder Abuse field, victims of abuse are conceptualized as old, frail, and dependent. Definitions of elder abuse are highly contested, but most include the physical, sexual, psychological, and financial abuse of older people, usually taking place in a domestic or institutional context (McCreadie, 1996).

In this discussion, we have chosen to use broad internationally recognized working definitions of elder abuse and violence against women.

> *Elder abuse is defined as a single or repeated act, or lack of appropriate*
> *action, occurring within a relationship where there is an expectation of trust,*
> *which causes harm or distress to an older person.*
> *Action on Elder Abuse, quoted by WHO/INPEA (2002)*

In addition to specifying age but not gender, this definition differs from a definition of violence against women in that the victim-perpetrator relationship is characterized as one of trust. The term "violence against women" refers to many types of harmful behaviors directed at women and girls because of their sex. As defined in Article 1 of the United Nations *Declaration on elimination of violence against women*, these include:

> *... any act of gender-based violence that results in, or is likely to result in,*
> *physical, sexual, or psychological harm or suffering to women, including*
> *threats of such acts, coercion, or arbitrary deprivation of liberty, whether*
> *occurring in public or private life.*
> *United Nations (1993)*

Obviously, there is nothing in the UN statement that implies that women of any age are excluded from this definition. At a family or individual level, both definitions point to acts of physical abuse, financial abuse, neglect, psychological abuse, sexual assault, and violations of human rights (Hightower et al., 2001).

As stated in the *Beijing Declaration*:

> *In all societies, to a greater or lesser degree, women and girls are subjected*
> *to physical, sexual, and psychological abuse that cuts across lines of income,*
> *class, and culture.*
> *United Nations (1995, paragraph 113)*

An epidemiological report from the School of Public Health, Johns Hopkins University (Heise et al., 1999) suggests that research and advocacy activities demonstrate growing consensus that abuse of women and girls is best understood within a gender framework because this abuse stems in part from the subordinate status in society of women and girls.

At the international level, the need to develop and maintain a gender perspective on later life is central to the Madrid International Plan of Action on Ageing (MIPAA) (United Nations, 2002). The agenda it sets out pays particular attention to gender issues in developing an understanding and responding to abuse of older adults. The Secretary General acknowledged the role of both sexism and ageism as contributing factors in the abuse of older adults (United Nations, 2002).

In September 2002, the UN Economic Commission for Europe, of which Canada is a member state, approved a Regional Implementation Strategy for the Madrid Plan (United Nations Economic Commission for Europe, 2002a, 2002b). Incorporating a gender perspective in all aging policies is one of several priority areas identified in that strategy. Next, the Toronto Declaration on the Global Prevention of Elder Abuse (WHO/University of Toronto & Ryerson University/INPEA, 2002) recognized that women are particularly vulnerable to abuse in later life and urged those working in the field of elder abuse to "consider a gender perspective" (p. 3).

Two inter-linked silos

In the 1960s, a powerful social movement of women developed in Western societies to further women's rights. An American writer who was influential in this movement noted "It is a movement that some call 'feminist' but should more accurately be called humanist; a movement that is an integral part of rescuing this country from its old, expensive patterns of elitism, racism, and violence" (Steinem, 1970). From this social movement, in response to what we knew then as "woman battering," "domestic violence," or "spousal violence," there emerged a strong grassroots response. Women came together in the 1970s and 1980s to support battered women, provide emergency shelter, and offer support services. As women gained greater understanding of the dynamics of power and control that dominated the lives of many women in their homes, they lobbied and advocated for a public response to this issue. Gradually, violence in intimate relationships was reframed, from a private family matter to a crime that the state has an obligation to address (Brandl et al., 2003; Hightower et al., 2001).

Abuse of older adults, or "elder abuse" as it is known within the professional and academic literature, was first recognized as "granny bashing," a label that is clearly gender specific. It was first identified and described in British scientific journals in the mid-1970s (Baker, 1977; Burston 1975), shortly after Erin Pizzey (1974) published her groundbreaking book, a graphic exposure of wife battering, entitled *Scream Quietly or the Neighbors Will Hear*.

This first acknowledgment of abuse in later years occurred somewhat in tandem with actions to address domestic violence. But "granny bashing" quickly became "elder abuse" and gender-neutral as it became a subject of academic research and professional practice. Penhale (1999) acknowledges that early research on elder abuse was not particularly concerned with gender and could be described as either "gender absent" or "gender-neutral." She notes that early elder abuse researchers failed to even consider gender as a factor of relevance in situations of elder abuse. Gender-neutrality ignores systemic explanations grounded in structural power differences between women and men and that challenge abusive behavior. It also has the effect of neutralizing the fact that older women experience abuse more than men (Penhale, 1999).

What were the factors that influenced this gradual move to a gender-neutral framework? Was it a reaction to the growth of feminism? Was it the social values and perspectives of the mostly male researchers? Or was it because the dominant assumption in an ageist society is that old age means dependency and diminished competence? This is a stereotyped picture of aging in which the elderly are sexless, and males and females are indistinguishable. Those who are older are seen as losing their faculties, beauty, energy, memory, and creativity, and also their value to society. The term *elder abuse* seems to reflect a societal predisposition to homogenize older people by not taking into account individual differences and gender.

Harbison (1999) makes the point that like child abuse, social and health care professionals identified elder abuse as a concern. These professionals are used to diagnosing a problem and prescribing a solution. Consultation with the client or patient is not a large part of the process. Given this medical model approach, it is not surprising that there has been limited community consultation with older adults about the issue. Until very recently, older adults have not been included in research or prevention activities. Like children, older adults have been seen as unable to, unwilling to, or perhaps cannot be trusted to make appropriate decisions for themselves, so others need to make decisions on their behalf. This model is uncomfortably close to blaming the victim, and attributes the mental difficulties of a small minority of older adults to everyone of similar age. This approach has resulted in legislation, services, and support that appear to be modeled on child abuse services (Harbison, 1999; Sacco, 1990; Vinton, 1999). This is a process that violates cardinal points of the UN Principles for Older Persons: independence, participation, care, self-fulfillment, and dignity (United Nations, 1991).

In contrast to abuse in later life, violence and abuse of younger women was identified through the women's movement and incorporated into that movement as a social problem and as an aspect of larger issues of gender discrimination and inequality. An important principle in the philosophy of the movement has been that hearing from victims and survivors is an essential element in addressing the problem. This has certainly been a key factor in the development of grassroots advocacy and services for younger battered women and their children. The main response to gender violence and discrimination in younger years has been through the advocacy and actions of women.

In Canada and elsewhere, this has been characterized by volunteer advocacy; community-based services, including shelters and safe homes; and in recent years through lobbying at local, national, and international political bodies. The predominantly young women who were the leaders within the women's movement in its early days would have had the beliefs and the strength to resist efforts by anyone outside of the movement to take over "their" problem. While there is a significant body of work that examines the gendered nature of violence and abuse in women's lives through their reproductive years, in the case of elder abuse, there has been little analysis by feminists that examines ageism and the gender biases and types of violence that are present in the lives of older women. Much of the research on women's human rights in regard to equality and social justice ignores the realities of the lives of many older women. Is it ageism that blocks contemporary attention to these issues or ageism and sexism?

The failure to recognize the gendered nature of abuse of older women cannot be solely attributed to researchers and practitioners in the field of elder abuse. Those working in the field of violence against women must accept a large share of that responsibility. Until very recently, there has been a failure by both fields to deal with the ageist assumptions implied in not recognizing and not addressing the gendered nature of much of the abuse in the lives of older women.

The common myth persists that victims of "violence against women" are young women, often with babies or toddlers, living with abusive partners (Hightower, 2004). A dozen years ago, Aitken and Griffin (1996) made the point in their discussion of gender and abuse in later life that a notable aspect of the way feminists had addressed violence against women was to unconsciously separate older women from the women of younger ages whose issues they addressed. This was not explicitly stated nor recognized but was implicit in their work.

The reality is that there is confusion over the distinction between domestic violence and elder abuse, the result of which is that older women's needs are overlooked by women's services and by those responding to abuse in later years (Hightower et al., 2001; Morgan Disney et al., 2000; Olle, 2005; Scott et al., 2003). The other important fact is that given their life experience, these women are less likely to report their experiences than other age groups. Women born before or during World War II were socialized during an era of strong beliefs about male and female roles. Marriage was "until death do us part." Leaving a marriage for any reason was just not sanctioned. You just made the best of life circumstances. Family matters stayed private. Domestic violence was not a crime. Many women just suffered in silence. As older woman said, "You just got on with it" (Scott et al., 2003). There are women today who do not actively seek help from women's services, health professionals, or the police. This is gradually changing, at least in Canada and other western societies, with the passing of the older generation and the aging of the young women who were activists in the 1960s, with slow progress toward improvements in criminal justice policy and practices, and with more and better research on family violence.

Qualitative and participatory research is becoming accepted as valid, and there are more researchers in the field of violence against women focusing on abuse of older women, and quantitative research in the area of elder abuse is increasingly reporting on gender differences.

Quantitative and qualitative research: a snapshot

In recent years, researchers on abuse in later life are increasingly reporting that the majority of older victims of violence and abuse are women and that the majority of perpetrators are male (Boyack et al., 1995; Brownell et al., 1999; Crichton et al., 1999; Dunlop et al., 2000; Lachs et al., 1997; Lithwick et al., 1999; Pittaway and Gallagher, 1995; Statistics Canada, 2006). Perpetrators are husbands, partners, sons, or grandsons.

A study published in 2004 in the *American Journal of Public Health* begins to fill what has been a serious gap in the medical science research literature. In this paper, Mouton and his colleagues examine prevalence and incidence (over three years) of abuse among older (postmenopausal age) women. Their data from nearly 92,000 women ages 50 to 79 showed that 10,200 of those women had been abused at some time in the past year. A follow-up three years later added more than 2,400 more women who reported abuse in the intervening three years but had not in the initial survey year. The nature of the sample does not permit statistical estimates of incidence or prevalence in any general population of American women, so perhaps it is best to say, as these authors did, that the rates of abuse are "similar" for younger and older women. This study is important because it "involves perhaps the largest sample of functionally independent older women ever used for a study about abuse in this population," and, "to date, no study has examined the [statistical] associations with physical and verbal abuse in functionally independent, cognitively intact, older women" (Mouton et al., 2004, p. 605).

Mouton and colleagues also "acknowledge the role of gender in experiencing abuse, noting that women 65 years or older are more likely than older men to be victims of all forms of abuse except abandonment, even after adjusting for women comprising a larger proportion of the aging population. If a woman remains functionally independent, the risk factors for abuse mirror those for intimate partner violence" (Mouton et al., 2004, p. 609) These authors' summary conclusion is that 50- to 80-year-old "women are exposed to abuse at similar rates to younger women; [and] this abuse poses a serious threat to their health" (abstract).

Qualitative research

There continues to be a conspicuous gap in the elder abuse literature involving survivors and their voices, while in the violence against women literature, there is a small but growing attention to violence against older women. This is reflected in a number of participatory research studies focusing on the lives of older abused women. These studies over the past 10 years have been undertaken primarily in Australia, Canada, England, Scotland, and the United States. Women shared their stories of abuse suffered from childhood through into their later lives (Alcalde, 2005; Blood, 2004; Hightower et al., 2001; Morgan Disney et al., 2000; Sargent and Mears, 2000; Scott et al., 2003). In these studies, older women spoke of current and past violence from their husbands, partners, and family members.

Qualitative research, says Pain (1999, citing Murphy and Longino, 1992), is seen as one way of allowing older adults to speak for themselves and to interpret their own lives, rather than inferring this from empirical indicators. Pain further suggests that elder abuse research in particular has been dominated by quantitative analyses, and many sources point to the need for in-depth research on individual cases to explore how abuse is structured and experienced within the context of people's lives. What has the abuse meant to them? How have they coped with or resisted it? (Aitken and Griffin, 1996; Whittaker, 1995). Case studies have proved to be important elements of the research on older women abuse. Through the qualitative studies we hear women share their experience of gendered violence. Violence has been or continues to be an ongoing fact of daily life, as it was for many in their childhood, adolescence, and child-bearing years and on into old age. Here is the way one front-line worker described her clients:

> *Most of these women struggle daily with their poor health, a multitude of medications, and the chronic pain of living 20–50 years of an abusive marriage relationship. Not forgetting either, their years of abuse in their family of origin, the systemic abuse of wars, separations, depressions, poverty, and sexual stereotyping, all of which were very much a reality for these women.*
> *Kemp (2005, personal communication)*

Policy and legislation

Elder abuse legislation in many North American jurisdictions requires reporting abuse of seniors, like abuse of children, to designated social services agencies. More generally in North America, public policy developed from elder abuse research in the 1970s and 1980s that portrayed the victim as a functionally impaired person of advanced age, with a caregiver responding to the stress of their situation with abusive behaviors (Sacco, 1990). In the United States, Wolf (2000) explained that the construction of elder abuse as a social problem was profoundly affected by the alignment of elder abuse with adult protective services and pre-existing stereotypes about aging. The response to this early research has resulted in the development of mandatory reporting laws in about three-fourths of the American states and in several Canadian provinces.

This legislation bears the distinctive hallmark of child protection statutes. It does not allow the adults who come under its mandate to exercise the rights of competent adults, such as the right to make informed choices. Older people are not children; they are adults. As such, they should have the right to liberty and to choose how to live (Gordon and Tomita, 1990; Wahl, 2004). Mandatory reporting and supervision of elder abuse victims reflects and reinforces ageist attitudes and a stereotype of older adults as frail, dependent, and incompetent.

In contrast, domestic violence was reframed from a private family matter to a crime that the state has an obligation to address. Here the criminal justice system is seen as a key player in addressing and preventing domestic violence. Later research in the elder abuse field that further revealed the continuation of spousal abuse into later life raises key questions about legislation, policy, and practice in the field of elder abuse. In particular, efforts to integrate prevention, treatment, or protection into more general domestic violence strategies are lacking (Sacco, 1990, citing Mastrocola and Morris, 1989).

> *Temporary shelters, the employment of legal sanction, and self-help groups intended to empower victims may have much more applicability than strategies that emphasize the victim's age.*
>
> Sacco (1990, p. 123)

Failing to integrate prevention, treatment, or protection of adults into the already-developed strategies to address domestic violence may reinforce ageist attitudes. That lack of integration:

> *... may send the wrong message first to members of the general public who are encouraged to think that the domestic violence ends at some point in middle age, and second, to members of helping communities who will be discouraged from recognizing the manifestation of domestic violence within older client groups.*
>
> Sacco (1990, p. 123)

Now, we are finding increasing numbers of older women victims of violence and abuse by their partners. Some of this is a continuation of domestic violence that began in earlier years, and some is occurring for the first time in a new relationship in later life. Because of the disconnect that exists between elder abuse and violence against women, these women are not well served. As the elder abuse model puts emphasis on "caregiver stress," practitioners using this paradigm may assume the victim is the stressor and suggest that she should be more compliant and accommodating, thus presuming motivations that have nothing to do with the perpetrator's behavior. What she should be offered is empathy, emergency shelter, safety planning, advocacy, and empowerment, and the use of the criminal and civil justice systems (Hightower et al., 2001; Morgan Disney et al., 2000; Scott et al., 2003).

When abuses of older people are not treated as crimes, and the majority are crimes, we in effect remove them from the criminal justice system. The rationale provided is that older people are more in need of care and protection, that the criminal justice process is too stressful for them, and that anyway, most of the perpetrators are family members, so the victim will not want to prosecute them. This rationalization detracts from the criminality of the perpetrator and implies that because of age, an adult does not merit the same protections under the law as everyone else. So one might ask, where does the obligation of the state lie? How will we ever prevent violence in later life if perpetrators are not held accountable? This holds true in terms of the gendered nature of particular forms of violence perpetrated against older women (Kinnear and Graycar, 1999; Olle, 2005).

Conclusion

This chapter opened by suggesting that the gender-neutral focus of the field of elder abuse misses the key fact that abuse and violence in old age is not gender free or necessarily age-specific but rather is part of a continuum of violence across the lifespan. The "elder abuse" label actually reflects a societal ageist attitude that homogenizes older people by ignoring differences, including gender. In the same respect, those that work to address issues of violence against women within a feminist model of theory and practice ignore the reality of older women who may continue to experience gender-based violence, often intimate partner violence, until their death or the death of the perpetrator (Olle, 2005).

> While the focus of much of the work on violence and abuse suffered by older women has been within the family setting, it is important to remember it cannot be separated from the broader experience of the lives of women in later life. Issues come up over and over again around legislation, policy, and practice concerning human rights, attitudes, and stereotypes. Ageism plus sexism places abused older women in a triple jeopardy position in respect to access to adequate income, shelter, health care, and the quality of life.
>
> Gutman (2005, p. 23)

Violence and abuse happens in childhood, adulthood, and old age, and it is important that we do not isolate ourselves from colleagues addressing abuse at different stages of life. We must connect, learn from each other, and understand the impact of violence and abuse across the life span. Researchers who have conducted qualitative studies with older women hear over and over again stories of abuse from childhood on into later life. They hear of the impact of this abuse on their children's lives. At times, they hear of the abuse suffered by older women's husbands at the hands of their fathers.

The development of approaches to deal with these two inter-related issues, abuse in later life and violence against women, reflect their different origins. The latter, a community-based and community-driven response that emphasizes victim input, developed from a social movement. The former is a prescriptive response to presumed frailty or incompetence.

In terms of abuse in later life, gender is as important a variable as it is throughout life. Older adults are indeed heterogeneous, and age and gender continue to be major structural factors affecting our perception and responses to abuse in later life.

The gender-neutral focus on abuse in later life is gradually changing. More researchers and community women services in Canada are beginning to recognize that some women bring to old age a past history of control, domination, physical harm, sexual abuse, humiliation, and degradation that may continue in later life at the hands of a partner or adult children (Hightower et al., 2001; McCullough, 2000; Zink, 2005). Iborra Marmolejo echoed this in a recent study on elder abuse in Spain, stating that being a woman is a high risk factor throughout life, including old age. She further notes use of:

> the term "gender-based violence", to refer to the violence suffered by women merely for being women.
>
> Iborra Marmolejo (2008)

In Canada, the cost of housing and other necessities stops many women and some men from leaving abusers on whom they are financially dependent. They continue to remain in abusive situations because they cannot find decent and affordable housing in their communities (Spencer, 2005). We also must not forget the labor market realities. Abused women in their fifties, ineligible for the government supports that become available by age 65, typically have lives that are far more bleak than those facing men of the same age. Because they have no choice, they often stay in abusive situations well into their senior years.

There is still much to be done worldwide to improve older women's lives. In some places, cultural mores and gender roles still severely restrict older women's everyday lives. At the official INPEA event marking World Elder Abuse Awareness Day held in Geneva in 2007, Steven Lewis spoke of women's experience in much of Africa of domestic violence, infection, hunger, and poverty. In addition, the realities of HIV/AIDS have made many African older women assume responsibility for care of adult children who are sick or for grandchildren whose parents are dead or are too ill to provide care.

In parallel with the false dichotomy between elder abuse and domestic violence (Payne, 2008), qualitative and quantitative research on older woman abuse exist in separate realms, one relatively well-funded and published in prestigious journals, the other largely contributed by practitioners and their service agencies. What is said within these silos is not inherently contradictory, as their slices of truth are grounded in common realities. Could not better integration of these improve practice and people's lives?

References

Aitken, L., Griffin, G., 1996. Thinking in numbers—the feminization of old age and its conditions. In: Aitken, L., Griffin, G. (Eds.), Gender Issues in Elder Abuse. Sage, London.

Alcalde, J., 2005. Working toward best practices in responding to the abuse of older women in Ontario. In: Hightower, J., Smith, M.J., Hightower, H.C. (Eds.), Proceedings of Building Bridges for the Prevention of Older Woman Abuse: A Forum for Dialogue. BC/Yukon Society of Transitions Houses, Vancouver, BC, pp. 40–42.

Baker, A.A., 1977. Granny battering. Mod. Geriatr. 5 (8), 20–24.

Blood, I., 2004. Older Women and Domestic Violence. Help the Aged, London.

Boyack, V.J., McKenzie, L.M., Hansell, E.K., 1995. Synergy II: A Demonstration Project to Address the Issues of Violence in Older Families. Kerby Centre, Calgary, AB.

Brandl, B., Hebert, M., Rozwadowski, J., Spangler, D., 2003. Feeling safe, feeling strong: support groups for older abused women. Violence Against Women 9, 1490–1503.

Brownell, P., Berman, J., Salmone, A., 1999. Mental health and criminal justice issues among perpetrators of elder abuse. J. Elder Abuse Negl. 11, 81–94.

Burston, G.R., 1975. Granny bashing. Br. Med. J. 3 (6), 592.

Crichton, S.J., Bond, J.B., Harvey, C.D.H., Ristock, J., 1999. Elder abuse: feminist and ageist perspectives. J. Elder Abuse Negl. 10 (3/4), 115–130.

Dunlop, B.D., Rothman, M.B., Condon, K.M., 2000. Elder abuse: risk factors and use of case data to improve policy and practice. J. Elder Abuse Negl. 12, 95–122.

Gordon, R.A.M., Tomita, S., 1990. The reporting of elder abuse and neglect: mandatory or voluntary?. In: Roesch, R., Dutton, D., Sacco, V.F. (Eds.), Family Violence: Perspectives on Treatment, Research, and Policy. B.C. Institute on Family Violence, Burnaby, BC.

Gutman, G., 2005. Older women abuse in the context of population aging: issues, trends, traps and opportunities. In: Hightower, J., Hightower, H. (Eds.), Proceedings of Building Bridges for the Prevention of Older Woman Abuse: A Forum for Dialogue. BC/Yukon Society of Transition Houses, Vancouver, BC, pp. 22–32.

Harbison, J., 1999. The changing career of "elder abuse and neglect" as a social problem in Canada: learning from feminist frameworks? J. Elder Abuse Negl. 11 (4), 59–80.

Heise, L., Ellsberg, M., Gottemoeller, M., 1999. Ending Violence Against *Women Population Reports*, Series L, Number 11. Johns Hopkins University School of Public Health, Population Information Program, Baltimore, MD.

Hightower, J., 2004. Age, gender and violence: abuse against older women. Geriatr. Aging 7 (3), 60–64.

Hightower, J., Smith, M.J., Hightower, H.C., 2001. Silent and Invisible: A Report on Abuse and Violence in the Lives of Older Women in British Columbia and Yukon. BC/Yukon Society of Transition Houses, Vancouver, BC.

Iborra Marmolejo, I., 2008. Elder abuse in the family in Spain. Queen Sofia Center for the Study of Violence, Valencia.

Kinnear, P., Graycar, A., 1999. Abuse of Older People: Crime or Family *Dynamics Trends and Issues*. Australian Institute of Criminology, Canberra.

Lachs, M.S., Williams, C., O'Brien, S., Hurst, L., Horwitz, R., 1997. Risk factors for reported elder abuse and neglect: a nine-year observational study. Gerontologist 37 (4), 469–474.

Lewis, S., 2007. Abuse of older women within the context of the aids epidemics in Africa. World Elder Abuse Awareness Day Conference, Geneva, 15 June 2007. As reported in INPEA Bulletin, August 2007. <http://www.inpea.net>

Lithwick, M., Beaulieu, M., Gravel, S., 1999. Mistreatment of older adults: perpetrator-victim relationships and interventions. J. Elder Abuse Negl. 11 (4), 95–112.

McCreadie, C., 1996. Elder Abuse: An Update on Research. HMSO, London.

McCullough, A., 2000. A Handbook for Older Women Who Have Survived Abuse. Older Women's Long-Term Survival Society (OWLS), Calgary, AB.

Morgan Disney & Associates, Leigh Cupitt & Associates & Council on the Ageing (2000), Two Lives—Two Worlds: Older People and Domestic Violence, vols. 1–2. Office of the Status of Women, Canberra.

Mouton, C.P., Rodabough, R.J., Rovi, S.L.D., Hunt, J.L., Talamantes, M.A., Brzyski, R.G., Burge, S.K., 2004. Prevalence and 3-year incidence of abuse among post-menopausal women. Am. J. Public Health 94 (4), 605–612.

Olle, L., 2005. Older women and mental health. Women's Mental Health 7, 4.

Pain, R., 1999. Theorizing age in criminology: the case of home abuse. Br. Criminol. Conf. 2.d.

Payne, B.K., 2008. Training adult protective services workers about domestic violence: training needs and strategies. Violence Against Women 14 (10), 1199–1213.

Penhale, B., 1999. Bruises on the soul: older women, domestic violence, and elder abuse. J. Elder Abuse Negl. 11 (1), 1–22.

Pittaway, E., Gallagher, E.M., 1995. A Guide to Enhancing Services for Abused Older Canadians. British Columbia Office for Seniors, Victoria, BC.

Pizzey, E., 1974. Scream Quietly or the Neighbors Will Hear. Penguin, Harmondsworth.

Sacco, V.F., 1990. Elder abuse policy: an assessment of categoric approaches. In: Roesch, R., Dutton, D., Sacco, V.F. (Eds.), Family Violence: Perspectives on Treatment, Research, and Policy. B.C. Institute on Family Violence, Burnaby, BC.

Sargent, M., Mears, J., 2000. Older Women Speak Up. University of Western Sydney, Campbelltown, NSW.

Scott, M., McKie, L., Morton, S., Seddon, E., Wasoff, F., 2003. Ye jus' hae t' dae it yersel': Older Women and Domestic Violence in Scotland. Health Scotland, Edinburgh.

Statistics Canada, 2006. Family Violence in Canada: A Statistical Profile 2005 Canadian Centre for Justice Statistics. Statistics Canada (annual series), Ottawa, ON.

Spencer, C. 2005. Housing and senior abuse. Paper presented at the World Conference on the Prevention of Family Violence. October 23–26, Banff, Alberta.

Steinem, G. 1970. Interview Washington Post, Sunday June 7.

United Nations, 1991. United Nations principles for older persons. <http://www. un.org/esa/socdev/ageing/un_principles.html>

United Nations, 1993. Declaration on the elimination of violence against women General Assembly, 85th plenary meeting 20 December 48/104. <http://www. un.org/documents/ga/res/48/a48r104.htm>

United Nations, 1995. Fourth World Conference on Women Beijing Declaration and Platform for Action. <http://www1.umn.edu/humanrts/instree/e5dplw.htm>

United Nations, 2002. The second world assembly on ageing, Madrid. <http://www. un.org/swaa2002/>

United Nations Economic and Social Council, 2002a. Berlin ministerial decla-ration: a society for all ages in the UNECE Region. Report of the UNECE Ministerial Conference on Ageing, Berlin, 11–13 September. <http://www.bagso. de/mica/download/berl_md_e.pdf>

United Nations Economic and Social Council, 2002b. Regional implementation strategy for the Madrid International Plan of Action on Ageing 2002. UN, New York, NY.

Vinton, L., 1999. Working with abused older women from a feminist perspective. J. Women Aging 11 (2/3), 85–100.

Wahl, J., 2004. Legal issues: the case against adult protection legislation. Tor. Educ. Wife Assault Newsl. 13 (1), 18–19.

Whittaker, T., 1995. Violence, gender and elder abuse: towards a feminist analysis and practice. J. Gend. Stud. 4 (1), 35–45.

WHO/INPEA, 2002. Missing Voices: Views of Older Persons on Elder Abuse. World Health Organization, Geneva.

WHO/University of Toronto & Ryerson University/INPEA, 2002. The Toronto Declaration on the Global Prevention of Elder Abuse. World Health Organization, Geneva. <http://www.who.int/ageing/projects/elder_abuse/alc_toronto_declaration_en.pdf>

Wolf, R.S., 2000. Elders as victims of crime, abuse, neglect and exploitation. In: Rothman, M.B., Dunlop, B.D., Entzel, P. (Eds.), Elders, Crime and the Criminal Justice System: Myth, Perceptions, and Reality in the 21st Century. Springer, New York, NY.

Zink, T., 2005. The not so golden years: older women and intimate partner violence. In: Hightower, J., Smith, M.J., Hightower, H.C. (Eds.), Proceedings of Building Bridges for the Prevention of Older Woman Abuse: A Forum for Dialogue. BC/Yukon Society of Transitions Houses, Vancouver, BC, pp. 48–55.

3 The invisible problem of abused older men

Jordan I. Kosberg

This chapter emanates not from a male power perspective but rather from the realization that the abuse of older men is an invisible and under-studied problem. As such, there is a lack of knowledge regarding the abuse of older men that leads to a lack of needed community resources for them. This chapter presents an overview of the problem and offers suggestions for filling the gap between the existence of abuse of older men and the creation of preventive and interventive efforts for them. In the final analysis, a focus on the abuse of older men should be no more, but certainly no less, than a focus upon the abuse of older women.

Elder abuse as a woman's problem

It is not surprising that elder abuse has been primarily perceived to be a problem faced by older women. First of all, the great majority of older persons are women, numerically and proportionally, and the discrepancy in longevity between older women and older men increases by age group. As the existence of elder abuse is often the result of reports and surveys, it is not surprising that the number of older persons includes mainly older women.

Males are seen to be physically stronger than are women, and this extends to differences between older men and women. As older women are perceived to be, and often can be, less able to defend themselves and/or escape their abuse, so too are they believed to be more vulnerable to abusive acts. Sexual abuse of older persons is limited to older women, and such abuse against older men has not been discussed. The fact that men have been identified to be the main abusers of family members leads to the conclusion that, therefore, family victims of abuse are adult females or young boys or girls. Thus, if the perpetrators of intra-family violence (including elder abuse) are males, the victims must generally be females. The majority of discussions regarding victimization in society focuses upon men as abusers, criminals, and deviants (Kosberg, 2002), and the tendency to extrapolate to the perpetrators of elder abuse is not surprising.

Indeed, the image of females as victims and males as perpetrators is a very common theme carried in the popular press, professional literature, and the mass media. There has been a plethora of articles discussing the abuse of older women, but the discussion of abused older men is seldom in the press (Kosberg, 2002). This is also true for professional literature, whether in scholarly journals, books, or in presentations at conferences. The absence of attention on mistreatment against males leads to a conclusion that elder abuse is mainly, if not totally, perpetrated against older women. Moreover, in the mass media, such as television or movies, women are often portrayed as the victims of adversity. In addition, insulting and stigmatizing humor has often been directed to older men in the mass media (Kosberg, 1998). The notion of the "dirty old man" is not an uncommon phrase, whether said humorously by a comedian or inferred in a story plot. Lost in the popular movie, *Grumpy Older Men*, and its sequel, is the fact that such men are stereotyped in a negative and demeaning manner.

Older men are also seen to be privileged, compared to older women. They are believed to be in positions of power and authority within a marriage, family, or society. Such men are seen to have material or financial resources and to be the dispensers of such attributes to others in the family. This being the case, so it is reasoned, such "privileged" older men are in positions to control others in the family, such as wives and adult children. Such a perception of older men is not a result of empirical fact, for certainly the majority of older men are not affluent and powerful, and—indeed—such men might be dependent upon the members of their families. Yet, older women continue to be perceived as vulnerable and to be dependent upon "dominant" males (regardless of chronological age).

A final reason for the fact that elder abuse is perceived to be a woman's problem can be explained by the composition of those involved in community resources for older persons, in general, and for those who are abused, in particular. Empirical research findings and practice experiences consistently have found that the great majority of clients, patients, and program participants in most community services for older persons are women. Such is the case for abuse shelters, as well as in social and health care resources where abuse can be detected and treated (Kosberg, 1998). The fact is that many elder abuse shelters are located within women's shelters. The understandable lack of older males in such settings is incorrectly interpreted to be an indication that older men are not abused. Thus, for all these reasons, elder abuse has been perceived to be a problem of older women.

Findings regarding the abuse of older men

Although the number of older abused women exceeds the number of abused older men, this is not to suggest that the proportion of older women who are abused far exceeds the proportion of older men who are abused. Indeed, there is some suggestion that older men are as likely as are older women to be abused. In their study of elder abuse in Boston, Pillemer and Finkelhor (1988) found an equal number of abused older men and older women. Given the greater number of older women in the population, study results suggest an over-representation of older men who are abused. In a national study of elder abuse in the United States, Tatara (1993) also found that the proportion of older men who were abused exceeded the proportion of women who were abused.

One possible explanation for such findings is related to the fact that they are most likely to be living with a spouse within a family setting, which is the setting in which most elder abuse occurs. In 1977–1978, Steinmetz wrote of the "Battered Husband Syndrome," suggesting that husbands, including older husbands, might be especially vulnerable for being abused. Indeed, there has been a developing body of literature discussing the abuse of older husbands (McNeely and Robinson-Simpson, 1987; Pritchard, 2001; Tutty, 1999). Focusing on spouses, but also on other family members and personal relationships, Cook (1997), Nicolls and Dutton (2001), and Reeves et al. (2007) have discussed the abuse by women against male intimates.

There are several explanations for the abuse of older husbands (or "intimates"). A first reason will not generate great sympathy, but the fact is that some abused older husbands had abused their wives earlier in their marriages. An older wife might retaliate against her (formerly abusive) husband when he becomes older, more impaired, and vulnerable. There is some suggestion that older wives caring for impaired and dependent husbands may become resentful and angry and rate their relationships as unsatisfying (Wallsten, 2000). Should the older husband be a provocateur (i.e., ungrateful and overly demanding) and/or a former abuser, a wife who feels she is in an unsatisfying marriage and is especially burdened or depressed, might engage in acts of abusive omission or commission against the husband.

Abuse of older fathers has received some attention in the literature (Kosberg, 2005). In those families where a father may have control over finances or valued possessions, adult children may seek to influence the father's decisions regarding the distribution of his resources through intimidation, coercion, or manipulation. While the dependent role of older parents on their children has been a common theme in elder abuse literature, the fact remains that adult children may be dependent upon their older parents (especially older fathers) and make unwanted or excessive demands. Should the adult child be embarrassed at his or her dependency on the parent and angry that the parent does not provide that which is wanted, there is a possibility that elder abuse will occur.

An adult child who had suffered abuse by the father, and/or had observed their mother's abuse by the father, might be at high risk to abuse the father as he ages and becomes more impaired. The explanation for such inter-generational abuse includes the child's learned behavior while growing up, intentional retaliation against the earlier abuse by the father, and unconscious acts against the father.

Sexual abuse against older women has been discussed as one form of abuse; very little—if even that—has been written about such abuse of older men; at least not until Teaster and Roberto (2004) and Teaster et al. (2007) reported that older men who are mentally or physically challenged are vulnerable to sexual abuse. Some of these high-risk older men reside in congregate settings where they live in close proximity with specially challenged persons who might take advantage of the vulnerability of an older man. Sexual abuse against an older man can also occur within domestic settings where a vulnerable older man can be victimized by a relative (or non-relative) with mental retardation or other such challenges.

Special groups of vulnerable older men

Thus, there is evidence of the existence of elder abuse against men. The majority of such attention focused upon older men living within a family and being abused by a wife, adult child, and/or other family member. Yet, there are other groups of older men who are vulnerable to abuse who remain rather invisible (cf. Kosberg and Kaye, 1997).

Older men living in inner cities outnumber older women in such locations (Keigher, 1991). Such individuals can live in single room occupancy (SRO) facilities or in other congregate settings within inner cities. Others are homeless. It is not surprising that homeless older men, living on the street, within shelters, or in "squatter villages" in urban areas, might be especially vulnerable to abusive acts by younger inner-city dwellers (including homeless persons) and/or those who would prey upon such persons (Eckert and Repaci, 1997). The possibility of substance abuse and/or mental illness among homeless populations can be seen to exacerbate the vulnerability of older persons in such inner-city settings.

The aging of prison populations has received increased attention, if for no other reason than the health care costs to prison systems with a growing number of aging and elderly prisoners are seen to be excessive. In some states, nursing homes are being established on prison grounds. One solution to this situation is the involuntary discharge of older prisoners without necessary preparation or discharge plan for community-based living. There is a growing body of literature about the vulnerability of older prisoners to abuse and maltreatment (Formby and Abel, 1997; Stojkovic, 2007). Old age is seen to come earlier in such settings, as physical ability and strength is a daily requirement for survival and safety. Younger prisoners may prey upon vulnerable older prisoners. Undoubtedly, such abuse does occur within prison settings; yet, unfortunately, advocates for the prevention of elder abuse have seldom focused on older prisoners.

Rural populations are often deprived and impoverished, despite the popular image of the serene and close-knit life in rural areas (Bull, 1998). Little has been written about the quality of life for older persons in rural settings; less has been written about the importance of gender. Yet, there is reason to believe that older rural men are enjoying a lower quality of life than are older rural women. While for both older men and women living in rural areas, there are disadvantages resulting from a lack of resources to meet their needs, including transportation to get to social and health services, older men in rural areas have been found to be less involved with their families, including adult children. Inasmuch as families, in general but certainly within rural areas, have been found to help facilitate the use by elderly relatives of community resources, the lack of such informal assistance is seen to work against the linking of older men to needed community resources.

There is a body of knowledge regarding differences in the quality of life between those older men who are married and those who are not. Married men have been found to have higher levels of physical and psychological health, in part due to the efforts of their wives to link their husbands with needed community resources (Hooyman and Kiyak, 2005). Thus, those men who are not married (or who are not in a long-term relationship) do not fare as well as those who are, despite stereotypes depicting the social and romantic opportunities for unattached older men—given the preponderance of "available" older women (as well as those who are considerably younger). In fact, it has been found that these men who are alone are often lonely (and vulnerable) (Rubenstein, 1986). Loneliness can make such older men vulnerable to victimization by those who would prey on older men's desire for companionship, friendship, and affection. Some lonely older men might be especially vulnerable to bogus and misleading attention leading to economic abuse or other efforts to part them from their resources (Satariano, 1997). For example, a salesperson might feign friendship or a woman might fake romantic interest.

Older gay men may experience similar domestic violence as do older men in heterosexual relationships. But, in addition, there has been a lengthy body of literature discussing the fact that older gay men may be abused by younger gays, as well as by homophobics, who would take advantage of the advanced age of the homosexual male (Berger, 1984).

Self-abuse is among the most common form of elder abuse seen by those working in elder abuse agencies. In this regard, men, in general, and older men, in particular, who are depressed or face other types of emotional, physical, or economic challenges are at high risk to engage in self-destructive behavior (McIntosh et al., 1997). For example, there is a direct relationship between chronological age of males and their suicide rates. Males are more likely than women to use tobacco and to abuse alcohol, illegal drugs, and medications. In facing the challenges in the later years, it may well be that older men turn to more dangerous types of coping mechanisms (i.e., suicide, substance abuse) than do women (who are more likely to use problem-solving techniques or religion in dealing with their problems).

The invisibility of abused older men

There are several explanations for the "invisibility" of abused older men and the lack of attention given to them. First of all, the dearth of research on them is apparent, as is the lack of literature that discusses the possibility of abused older men. If there is little acknowledgment of the existence of the abuse of older men; *ipso facto*, there is no problem.

As was mentioned previously, older men are often located in rather "invisible" settings where their abuse will not be seen (and reported). Such settings include inner cities and rural areas, and within prisons, "homeless" shelters, halfway houses, boarding homes, and institutional settings (such as mental health facilities and long-term care facilities). The fact that there may be relatively few older men in some of these residential settings adds to the lack of awareness of their problems. Moreover, because older men are often found within domestic settings, their abuse is less likely to be witnessed by non-family members. Older men, living on the streets, are often a faceless group, and their mental illnesses, substance abuse, and impoverishment can lead to stigmatization that can be coupled with sexism and ageism. The result can be not only their invisibility but also their irrelevance to the larger community.

Older men who are abused by their wives or other members of the family might be charged, in some circumstances, as being the abuser should they resist, defend themselves, or seek to restrain the abusing person. Such a phenomenon has been labeled "reciprocal abuse." In such situations, the older man seeking to restrain the abusing person may, in the process, cause injury or be otherwise charged as the abuser. The possibility exists that there is no clear abuser or abused in some domestic violence. It is unknown, but suspected, that a proportion of domestic violence attributed to older husbands might be the result of such "reciprocal abuse."

There are many differences between older men and women in the use of formal services (including those available for the reporting and treating of abused persons). Males, in general, and older men, in particular, are much less likely than their female counterparts to use community resources (Courtenay, 2003). Thus, older men are much less likely to know how to report their adversities. They are likely to have little experience in accessing services that are available in the community. Older men, especially those living alone, facing physical or emotional challenges, will not use resources, and their problems will not be reported and documented. Thus, the abuse of older men remains under-counted in formal reports and in professional case records.

Abused older men or women fail to report their adversities for several possible reasons. Yet, gender role socialization of older men, raised in earlier periods of time and possibly in more traditional societies, leads them to view their problems in a different manner than do older women (Thompson, 2008). As will be discussed, older traditional men may accept their maltreatment in a stoic manner and not admit their abuse to others. In some instances, abused older men will believe that they are being "paid back" for their earlier acts of commission (abuse) or omission (neglect) of children or wives, and they will not report their adversities. Older men who have been financially abused by those who preyed upon their loneliness will be embarrassed at their vulnerability and may well fail to report the abuse. Fathers who were the heads of their households and who are abused by adult children may not wish to admit (to themselves and to others) that their adult children ill-respect them. Some older men will fail to admit facing adversity because they want to maintain the appearance of power and control in their family.

Explanations for the abuse of older men

Social values toward older men might give some clues for reasons for their abuse. These clues are based upon the author's assumptions. It is suspected that older men might be less valued in society than are older women or younger men. For example, compared to older mothers, it is believed that older fathers receive less concern and affection from their families. This will be related to the quality of the older father's earlier behavior toward family members.

It is believed that most societies give younger persons preference over older persons. Further, it is suspected that greater accord is given to older persons who have accomplished more in their lives (as measured in financial terms) than those who have not. In a similar way, older persons with families seem to be given greater recognition than those who are without families. Finally, it is suspected that urban populations are more highly regarded than those in rural areas of a country. Accordingly, it can be assumed that some older men—those who are without families, less affluent, and living in rural areas—might have less social regard and be more vulnerable to adversity at the hands of others. Obviously, to confirm such suspicions, empirical research is needed.

As mentioned, there is reason to believe that men who engaged in abusive behavior of family members earlier in their lives are at high risk for being abused in their later years. In such instances, the abuser becomes abused. Such inter-generational cycles of violence are often directed against the weakest members of the family, such as children, women, and the elderly. Certainly, the propensity for such intra-family violence can result from "learned behavior," and elder abuse can be targeted upon an earlier abuser: the husband/father. Recent writings (Bullock, 2005) also suggest that older grandfathers (alone or with their wives) can and do raise their grandchildren and that these custodial grandfathers may be vulnerable to abusive behavior by grandchildren who have physical, emotional, or social problems (Bullock, 2007; Kosberg and MacNeil, 2005).

If an older man had, or continues to have, financial resources, he might be at special risk for abuse. Earlier work on elder abuse had emphasized the dependent role of the older person economically, physically, and emotionally on others (most often the family). Yet, there has been increasing awareness that the younger members of the family might be dependent upon the elderly parents. The likelihood of such dependency of adult children might result from a multitude of reasons, such as unemployment and lost incomes, divorce or separation, child caring responsibilities, physical and emotional challenges, and addictions, among others. A parent with resources may support and/or house an adult child. In turn, the dependent adult child's feelings of guilt and embarrassment, and possible anger that the support given does not measure up to the child's expectations or needs, may evolve into abusive behavior toward the elderly parent. An elderly father who is seen to be overly demanding, insulting, or stingy might well be at high risk for abuse by such a dependent adult child.

Finally, older men can be considered as high risk for abuse as determined by high-risk indicators (Kosberg and Nahmiash, 1996). Older men are more likely to be married and live in domestic settings. Most husbands are older than their wives, so they will be more likely to be ill, impaired, and dependent upon their wives. Substance abuse of older persons has been identified as a predictor of possible adversity against them. Because men are more likely to abuse alcohol and drugs than women, it can be assumed that older men with such problems might be more likely to be abused in their later years. There has been some suggestion that the provocative nature of care recipients makes them more prone to abuse at the hands of their caregivers. Indeed, an overly demanding care recipient may exacerbate the problems faced by an already burdened (and angry) caregiver. There is also some evidence that older men are more likely to fight their dependency on others whether in the family or within long-term care facilities. Their efforts to maintain their independence, dignity, and control might be met with an inferior form of care (such as neglect or abuse) when compared to the care given to a more compliant care recipient.

Failure to use community services

Most of what is known about elder abuse results from national surveys, state Adult Protective Service (APS) reports (in the US), experiences by staff in formal social and health service settings, empirical research findings, and mass media. Much of the abuse against older men is invisible as a result of their own failure to get involved in the helping process. It is further believed that there may be both formal agency and professional staff biases against older men who are abused and maltreated (Kosberg, 2005).

It is possible that older men may not define the neglectful or abusive behavior they receive as elder abuse. They may, for example, see it as a form of retribution for their earlier behavior toward others (such as a spouse or child). If religious, these men might define their current treatment to be preordained, or otherwise meant to take place. If duped by an unscrupulous person, an older man may believe that he was to blame for his own stupidity or naivety. Thus, some abused older men might not believe themselves to be victimized or their situations worthy of reporting.

In fact, as a result of their earlier gender socialization, older men may have been taught not to admit having problems; rather, they should exemplify stoicism, self-reliance, and bravery in the face of such situations (Kaye, 1997). Thus, some older men—especially those from certain cultures where the norms of masculinity are especially strong—might be very reluctant to admit to being abused. So, too, will they be unwilling to seek out assistance for their adversities. It cannot be assumed that an older abused man will necessarily admit the problems that he faces to members of the family, to non-family members, or to those from health, social service, or law enforcement resources.

Both empirical research findings and practice experiences lead to the conclusion that men are less likely to use needed community services than are women (Tudiver and Talbot, 1999). While the previous discussion partially explains differences between older men and older women in defining problems and admitting having problems, there are also other explanations. In the first instance, there may not be resources available for older men. It is suspected that there are few community resources for abused older men (i.e., elder abuse shelters, treatment groups for abused husbands). Even if older men may not be formally excluded, they may be reluctant to become involved in programs and services that serve mainly older females or younger persons. In addition, when the program staff of a community resource is mainly—if not totally—composed of females, some older men may be reluctant to participate in such programs. This will be especially true for those men who feel uncomfortable sharing personal feelings (such as fears or hopes).

While the reasons for reluctance to confide with others might result from subjective feelings of these men, there is some suggestion of bias against older men held by those in the helping professions (Wisch et al., 1995). As had been mentioned, there are those who do harbor negative feelings toward older men as a result of earlier experiences (i.e., having an absent or abusing father). It is possible that such personal past events in the lives of formal care providers will affect their motivation to assist older males. A male professional having traditional masculine values may view an abused older man in a scornful manner (for being weak and dependent), and there is suggestion that traditional male professionals may feel uncomfortable with an older male client who appears unmanly or weak (Wisch and Mahlik, 1999). Perhaps, such professionals would have difficulty working with older men being abused in intimate (heterosexual or homosexual) relationships.

Combating the abuse of older men

There are several things that can be done to combat the invisible problem of older men who are abused. First of all, there is the need to publicize the existence of such problems. Advocates for the prevention of abused older persons, which should include a cross-section of society, need to use the mass media to ensure a widespread awareness of the existence of abused older men, and an understanding of the reasons for such abuse. Stereotypes should be challenged that portray men (including older men) as powerful and self-reliant, as well as the image of such men as partner abusers, "dirty old men," and absent fathers. Certainly, some men are or had been abusive, deviant, absent, and violent, but the great majority of men are not. Sensitizing citizens to the possibility and existence of elder abuse against men will also result in the awareness by abused older men that their plight is not unique, and that there can be assistance available in the community.

Because abuse of older men may result from the combination of their being men and being old, it is necessary to realize that a reduction in the abuse of older men may require the awareness and reduction of both ageism and sexism in society. Any belief that a person is inferior and less worthy on the basis of any attribute, including gender and age, is wrong. Accordingly, even those who advocate for the prevention of elder abuse must guard against ignoring or minimizing the abuse of older men.

As was mentioned, there has been evidence of bias and discrimination against older male clients, patients, and program participants by formal caregivers (regardless of their gender). The possible double bias of ageism and sexism has been found for non-professionals and professionals alike (Berger et al., 2005; Hatch, 2005). Accordingly, there is the need to focus attention on the education and training of those who are, or who will be, working in community resources that provide social, medical, and psychological assistance, among others, to older persons. It has been found that there has been little attention given to males, in general, and older males, in particular, in most professional education and training (such as in social work). The lack of attention to males, as well as their biased portrayal when they are discussed in professional literature, has already been described. Similarly, discussion of elder abuse as solely a female concern needs to be challenged and countered by a more balanced, and equitable, approach in the education and training of future and present staff working in the helping field.

The prevention of elder abuse of men is actually little different than the prevention of abuse of older women. Thus, there is a need to be assured that community resources are available to provide supportive assistance to the informal, mainly family, caregivers (who are found to be the group most likely to be the abusers of older persons).

Both preventive and interventive assistance is necessary for these caregivers who often care for older persons who are dependent, impaired, and vulnerable. As discussed, the possibility of caring for such individuals who are provocative adds to the vulnerability of such older persons. Whether the dependent older person is a husband or a wife, or a father or mother, is less important than the availability of caregiver assistance offered by community resources. Such assistance can include a range of services for the older care recipient (i.e., respite care, day care, visiting nurse) and for the caregiver (i.e., home care, support group, counseling).

Just as there is a need to consider supportive services for those who care for older persons, so too is there a need to consider alternatives for family caregiving. In some situations, the best alternative for an older person is not within the home of a relative. Indeed, there might be an abusive history or a disharmonious relationship; also the family might be already burdened by the needs of other family members (such as an unemployed major wage earner, an addictive child, or a specially challenged sibling). Placing an older person, regardless of gender, into such a family may well exacerbate the problems faced by the family. The possibility of abuse against the older person placed in such a family setting needs to be considered.

Advocacy for those older persons who live outside traditional family settings also needs to be considered. This chapter has identified invisible groups of older men, such as those who are homeless, incarcerated or institutionalized, live in rural areas, as well as those who are lonely and alone. It is believed that there are unmet advocacy needs for such "invisible" groups of older persons (that include women as well as men). It is suspected that there are advocacy efforts on behalf of younger members of such groups, but—with the exception of those institutionalized in long-term care facilities—such efforts generally have excluded older persons.

A final, and possibly most important, method by which to combat the abuse of older men is by assessing the community resources that exist for abused older persons. There is a need to ensure that such resources will meet the needs of both abused older men and abused older women. While such equity might officially exist, it is necessary to ensure a proportionally balanced usage rate for older women and older men. If not, there will be a need to consider such things as the focus of publicity, the need for outreach efforts, consideration of referral sources, and staff characteristics, among other things (Kaye and Crittenden, 2005). It has been found, for example, that outreach by older males can be especially effective in recruiting older male clients to a program or service.

Conclusion

There is a need to be mindful that elder abuse is perpetrated against older men as well as older women. Efforts are needed to raise the level of awareness and concern in this regard. More community and national surveys are necessary to empirically support assumptions about the existence of abused older men. Studies are needed to learn more about invisible groups of older men who are vulnerable to the possibility of elder abuse. Further knowledge is needed to better understand the reasons (causes) for the abuse of older men.

In addition, community services for older persons, in general, and for those focusing on abused older persons, in particular, need to assess the characteristics of their client and patient populations to determine if older men as well as older women are being adequately served. Discrepancies in usage rates require reconsideration of planning and service delivery, and the possible need for the creation of new efforts to reach and serve older abused men.

Underlying equity in service provision for abused older women and older men is the consideration of gender equity in our values and attitudes. In a concern for the prevention of the abuse of older men, we will need to advocate for vulnerable groups of men who presently do not have advocates, such as those who are homeless, incarcerated, institutionalized, alone, and in rural locations, among others. But, so too, our efforts in advocating for the prevention of abused older men focuses upon loved ones: our fathers, grandfathers, brothers, and—in the future—our sons and grandsons.

Thus, it is believed, that those who advocate for the prevention of elder abuse need to consider both the abuse of older men as well as older women. In this, we should have both a personal as well as professional stake for preventing the abuse of older men. Such an effort should be no more, but certainly no less, than such an effort to prevent the abuse of older women.

References

Berger, R., 1984. The realities of gay and lesbian aging. Soc. Work 29, 57–62.

Berger, J.M., Levant, R., McMillan, K.K., 2005. Impact of gender role conflict, traditional masculinity ideology, alexithymia, and age on men's attitudes toward psychological help seeking. Psychol. Men & Masculinity 6 (1), 73–78.

Bull, C.N., 1998. Aging in rural communities. Natl. Forum 78 (2), 38–42.

Bullock, K., 2005. Grandfathers and the impact of raising grandchildren. J. Sociol. Soc. Welfare 32 (1), 43–59.

Bullock, K., 2007. The vulnerability for elder abuse among a sample of custodial grandfathers: an exploratory study. J. Elder Abuse Negl. 19 (3/4), 133–150.

Cook, P.W., 1997. Abused Men: The Hidden Side of Domestic Violence. Praeger Press, Westport, London.

Courtenay, W.H., 2003. Key determinants of the health and well-being of men and boys. Int. J. Men's Health 2 (1), 1–30.

Eckert, J.K., Repaci, L.G., 1997. Elder men in the inner city. In: Kosberg, J.I., Kaye, L.W. (Eds.), Elderly Men: Special Problems and Professional Challenges. Springer, New York, NY, pp. 54–73.

Formby, W.A., Abel, C.F., 1997. Elderly men in prison. In: Kosberg, J.I., Kaye, L.W. (Eds.), Elderly Men: Special Problems and Professional Responsibilities. Springer, New York, NY, pp. 98–112.

Hatch, L.R., 2005. Gender and ageism. Generations 29 (3), 19–25.

Hooyman, N.R., Kiyak, H.A., 2005. Social Gerontology: A Multidisciplinary Perspective, seventh ed. Allyn & Bacon, New York, NY.

Kaye, L.W., 1997. Service utilization and support provision of caregiving men. In: Kosberg, J.I., Kaye, L.W. (Eds.), Elderly Men: Special Problems and Professional Responsibilities. Springer, New York, NY, pp. 359–378.

Kaye, L.W., Crittenden, J.A., 2005. Principles of clinical practice. J. Sociol. Soc. Welfare 32 (1), 99–123.

Keigher, S.M. (Ed.), 1991. Housing Risks and Homelessness Among the Urban Elderly. Haworth Press, New York, NY.

Kosberg, J.I., 1998. The abuse of elderly men. J. Elder Abuse Negl. 9 (3), 69–88.

Kosberg, J.I., 2002. Heterosexual males: a group forgotten by the profession of social work. J. Sociol. Soc. Welfare 29 (3), 51–70.

Kosberg, J.I., 2005. Meeting the needs of older men: challenges for those in helping professions. J. Sociol. Soc. Welfare 32 (1), 9–31.

Kosberg, J.I., MacNeil, G., 2005. The elder abuse of custodial grandparents: a hidden phenomenon. In: Podneiks, E., Kosberg, J.I., Lowenstein, A. (Eds.), Elder Abuse: Selected Papers from the Prague World Congress on Family Violence. Haworth Press, New York, NY, pp. 33–53.

Kosberg, J.I., Nahmiash, D., 1996. Characteristics of victims and perpetrators and milieus of abuse and neglect. In: Baumhover, L.A., Beall, S.C. (Eds.), Abuse, Neglect, and Exploitation of Older Persons. Health Professions Press, Baltimore, MD, pp. 31–49.

McNeely, R.L., Robinson-Simpson, G., 1987. The truth about domestic violence: a falsely framed issue. Soc. Work November/December, 485–490.

McIntosh, J.L., Pearson, J.L., Lebowitz, B.D., 1997. Mental disorders of elderly men. In: Kosberg, J.I., Kaye, L.W. (Eds.), Elderly Men: Special Problems and Professional Challenges. Springer, New York, NY, pp. 193–215.

Nicolls, T.L., Dutton, D.G., 2001. Abuse committed by women against male intimates. In: Brothers, B.J. (Ed.), The Abuse of Men. Haworth Press, New York, NY, pp. 41–57.

Pillemer, K.A., Finkelhor, D., 1988. The relevance of elder abuse: a random sample survey. Gerontologist 28 (1), 51–57.

Pritchard, J., 2001. Male Victims of Elder Abuse: Their Experiences and Needs. Jessica Kingsley Publishers, London.

Reeves, K.A., Desmarais, S.L., Nicholls, T.L., Douglas, K.S., 2007. Intimate partner abuse of older men: considerations for the assessment of risk. In: Kosberg, J.I. (Ed.), Abuse of Older Men. Haworth Maltreatment & Trauma Press, Binghamton, NY, pp. 7–27.

Rubenstein, R.L., 1986. Singular Paths: Older Men Living Alone. Columbia University Press, New York, NY.

Satariano, W.A., 1997. The physical health of older men: the significance of the social and physical environment. In: Kosberg, J.I., Kaye, L.W. (Eds.), Elderly Men: Special Problems and Professional Challenges. Springer, New York, NY, pp. 159–174.

Steinmetz, S.K., 1977–1978. The battered husband syndrome. Victimology 2, 499–509.

Stojkovic, S., 2007. Elderly prisoners: a growing and forgotten group within correctional systems vulnerable to elder abuse. J. Elder Abuse Negl. 19 (3/4), 97–117.

Tatara, T., 1993. Understanding the nature and scope of domestic elder abuse with the use of state aggregate data: summaries of the key findings of a national survey of state APS and aging agencies. J. Elder Abuse Negl. 5 (4), 35–59.

Teaster, P.B., Roberto, K.A., 2004. Sexual abuse of older adults: APS cases and outcomes. Gerontologist 44 (6), 788–796.

Teaster, P.B., Ramsey-Klawsnik, H., Mendiondo, M.S., Abner, E., Cecil, K., Tooms, M., 2007. From behind the shadows: a profile of the sexual abuse of older men residing in nursing homes. In: Kosberg, J.I. (Ed.), Abuse of Older Men. Haworth Maltreatment & Trauma Press, Binghamton, NY, pp. 29–45.

Thompson E.H., Jr., 2008. Gender matters: aging men's health. In a special issue on older men's health. Generations 32 (1), 5–8.

Tudiver, F., Talbot, Y., 1999. Why don't men seek help? Family physician's perspectives on help-seeking behavior in men. J. Fam. Pract. 48 (1), 47–52.

Tutty, L., 1999. Husband Abuse: An Overview of Research and Perspectives. The National Clearinghouse on Family Violence, Health Canada, Ottawa, ON.

Wallstein, S.S., 2000. Effects of caregiving, gender, and race on the health, mutuality, and social supports of older couples. J. Aging Health 12 (1), 90–111.

Wisch, A.F., Mahalik, J.R., 1999. Male therapists' clinical bias: influence of client gender roles and therapist gender role conflict. J. Couns. Psychol. 46 (1), 51–60.

Wisch, A.F., Mahalik, J.R., Hayes, J.A., Nutt, E.A., 1995. The impact of gender role conflict and counseling technique on psychological help seeking in men. Sex Roles: J. Res. 33 (1), 77–90.

4 Abuse of lesbian, gay, transgender, and bisexual elders

Chris Morrissey

When considering the issues of abuse and neglect of older adults, a segment of the population that may be even more invisible than the abused older males described by Kosberg in Chapter 3, are members of the lesbian, gay, transgender, and bisexual (LGTB) community.

There has been little research conducted in Canada concerning the needs or experiences of aging or older LGTB people. "The health and social service needs of gay and lesbian elders and their families in Canada," carried out by researchers at McGill University (Brotman et al., 2003, 2006a), is the only national study. In Phase 1, conducted in 2000, focus groups were held in three Canadian provinces: Quebec, Nova Scotia, and British Columbia. Participants consisted of older gay and lesbian activists working within the gay/lesbian community, health care providers and policymakers within the public health system, and representatives of seniors groups. In Phase 2, which took place between 2003 and 2006, 90 interviews were carried out with gay and lesbian seniors, their caregivers, and service providers. Questions addressed included:

- What are the experiences of gay and lesbian seniors in accessing health care services in the community?
- What are the experiences and perspectives of persons caring for gay and lesbian seniors?
- How well understood are the needs, realities, and experiences of gay and lesbian seniors and their caregivers by health and social service providers? How well prepared is the health care sector to respond to these needs?

There have been a few other studies conducted that are regional or local in scope (e.g., Fritsch, 2005 studied service use in the Toronto area) or that focus on specific segments of the LGTB communities, particularly older lesbians. The latter include a study carried out by The Lesbian Seniors Care Society of Victoria, BC, and one currently in progress by the Réseau des LESBIENNES du Québec in conjunction with the Association de recherche IREF/UQÀM and Relais-Femmes (ARIR). To date there is very little, if any, empirical data available on aging of older Canadian transsexuals. However, anecdotal information is becoming available as LGTB individuals who have been part of the liberation movement become elderly themselves.

Impact of history

For centuries, individuals who engaged in same-sex activity were excommunicated or expelled from Judeo-Abrahamic religious traditions and identified as sinners. The criminal justice system in Canada treated sexual activity between members of the same sex as a criminal offense until 1969. From 1952 until 1973, homosexuality was included in the *Diagnostic and Statistical Manual of Mental Disorders* as a mental disorder.[1]

The historic realities just described have subjected *all* LGTB people to both homo/trans/biphobia and heterosexism. As a result of threats of imprisonment, institutionalization, loss of jobs, and ostracization from family and society, many LGTB people, especially older members, have learned to keep their sexual orientation and/or gender identity secret. These actions are abusive. They also create fertile ground for abuse and neglect. Aging and older LGTB people have experienced such abuse throughout their lives in varying degrees.

Internalized homo/trans/biphobia

As with all oppressed groups, most older LGTB individuals have internalized negative feelings about their own sexual orientation or gender identity. Some LGTB people entered into heterosexual marriages in their earlier years either because it was expected of them or as an attempt to convince themselves that they were not gay or lesbian. For some it was an attempt to ignore their gender identity concerns. Some older individuals may only be coming to terms with their sexual orientation or gender identity in their later years. At great cost to themselves, others have denied their sexual orientation or gender identity and have even exposed other LGTB people to divert interest in their orientation. Such actions are examples of both homophobia and internalized homophobia.

Interpersonal abuse

It is generally accepted that the issue of violence in interpersonal relationships happens as a result of a difference in power. In heterosexual relationships, it is the gender difference that can result in the power imbalance.

[1]Editors' note: As a result of controversy and protests by gay activists at American Psychiatric Association (APA) annual conferences from 1970 to 1973, and the emergence of new data from researchers such as Alfred Kinsey and Evelyn Hooker, the seventh printing of the DSM-II, in 1974, no longer listed homosexuality as a category of disorder. The diagnosis was replaced with the category of "sexual orientation disturbance." In 1980, in the DSM-III, that category was replaced with the diagnosis of "Ego-dystonic sexual orientation|ego-dystonic homosexuality" (Spitzer, 1981), which was removed in 1987 with the release of the DSM-III-R. A category of "sexual disorder not otherwise specified" continues in the DSM-IV-TR, which may include "persistent and marked distress about one's sexual orientation."

So what about relationships where the individuals are of the same gender? Does this mean that there is no such thing as violence in same-sex relationships? This is a myth. As in all personal relationships, there is always the possibility of violence in same-sex relationships. The fact that many older adults in same-sex relationships have lived in "the closet" increases a person's vulnerability. The threat of "outing" a partner to children, grandchildren, or authorities can be used as a means of maintaining control by partners in a same-sex relationship. Frequently, there is an additional shame factor for the victim. As a result of such circumstances, there is a diminished possibility of such violence being reported. If reported, service providers may not have the skills to respond appropriately. It is also possible for service providers to inadvertently "out" a client with serious consequences.

Exploitation

Older, closeted LGTB people can be exploited by children, caregivers, and others who are cognizant of their sexual orientation and/or gender identity. Gay men and transsexuals may be subject to exploitation by younger members of LGTB communities. Loneliness and ageism in the gay community provide fertile ground for exploitation. On the other hand, older gay men frequently reach out to younger men in the community, and such relationships can be interpreted as exploitation by workers.

Ageism in LGTB communities

In our society, all elders are subject to ageism. LGTB people also experience ageism from within the LGTB communities. As a result of pressures, "gay men might seek slimness and attractiveness, while lesbians tend to value strength and athletic vigor, but for both groups accepting the aging process presents a challenge." (glbtq encyclopedia of gay, lesbian, bisexual, transgender & queer culture). Images in LGTB publications are primarily those of young, fit, attractive men and, occasionally, women. Sexual currency is important for gay and bisexual men and "old" people regardless of sexual orientation are thought to be asexual. For gay men, this is a major challenge to their identity.

Homophobia = abuse and neglect

> *When the nurse realized that I was a lesbian, she no longer helped me get out of bed (65 year old lesbian after broken pelvis).*

Homo/trans/biphobia is the irrational fear and/or hatred of lesbian, gay, transgender, bisexual people. Dr Dorothy Riddle (1985), a psychologist from

Tucson, Arizona distinguishes four levels of homophobia: repulsion, pity, tolerance, and acceptance. An example of the latter is "You're not a lesbian to me, you're a person." Acceptance, in other words, implies that there is *something* to accept.

Homophobia still exists in many forms. Homophobia on the part of service providers is abusive. There are stories shared in LGTB communities, and there is the perception that this will be a common experience. This includes everything from refusal or denial of service to inadvertent comments. Comments such as "it doesn't matter to me if you are gay/lesbian/trans/bi," or "we treat all people the same" are examples of homophobia even when the service provider thinks she or he is expressing a positive attitude.

Heterosexism = systemic abuse and neglect

> *To me, hell on earth will be ending up in a straight-run residence or care home and being told by a sanctimonious staff member that I can't sleep with my partner, that I can't kiss or hold hands. That I can't discuss any gay topics with other residents, that I can't have gay material lying about, or that I can't watch gay videos.*
>
> Xtra West *letter to the editor, May 11, 2006*

Heterosexism is the privileging of heterosexuality over all other sexual orientations or identities. It is a way of subtly discriminating and oppressing sexual minorities. The effect is to create barriers and obstacles for LGTB people (Brotman et al., 2003). Heterosexism confirms and reinforces the need for LGTB people to remain in or retreat back into the closet or not to access programs or services available to them. This includes community-based programs available at senior centers as well as more specific health-related services: home support, seniors housing, assisted living, or residential care. A lifetime of experiences has led to generations of LGTB people having little to no faith in these systems to provide relevant services and care or to protect them from the homophobia of other participants or residents. The McGill study reinforces the fact that gays and lesbians fear and mistrust mainstream services. Transgender and transsexual people who have even less protection and resources have an even higher degree of fear and mistrust.

Heterosexism is a systemic form of abuse and neglect. It means that LGTB individuals are not able to access appropriate or relevant care. Heterosexism is evidenced by the *absence* of the following:

- Specific policies reflecting all aspects of diversity
- Diversity education, including specific LGTB education
- Forms that allow responses appropriate for a variety of sexual orientations or gender identities
- References to LGTB individuals or culture in written materials
- Images reflecting LGTB people and cultures

- LGTB visibility
- LGTB celebrations
- A welcoming environment for LGTB individuals

"Retiring back into the closet," an article in the *Globe and Mail* (Ambrose, 2006), reflects the concerns of aging and older LGTB people who are facing the need for receiving services from the seniors-serving sector. The primary concern is of isolation.

Two UK researchers, Holland and Rabbitt (1991), believe elderly people who have lost their independence simply prefer to talk about early experiences because their present lives are relatively uneventful. If telling stories of the past is a common reality for old people living in residential care, with whom can old LGTB individuals share their stories?

Policy issues

LGTB people are protected under Human Rights legislation. However, this does not guarantee the right to culturally relevant services. There is no public policy requiring services and agencies to actively end heterosexism. In the present climate, LGTB issues are frequently considered to be a low priority.

Several LGTB community agencies, including the LGTB Generations Project, actively work with the seniors-serving sector to support them with processes of organizational change and development.

The McGill Study recommends that agencies take the following steps to put A.S.T.O.P.P. to homophobia and heterosexism so that older LGTB individual will be able to receive culturally relevant services and care:

- Advocacy:
  - Develop sensitive residential and long-term care services.
  - Create the conditions for sensitive home care services.
  - Increase the visibility in social agencies and within the health care system.
- Social and Political Voice:
  - Ensure that wherever possible aging and older LGTB people's voices are heard and have the opportunity to contribute to the development of social and political policy.
  - Promote advocacy for elders.
  - Create empowering conditions for elders within social organizations.
  - Create opportunities for like-minded elders to meet socially.
  - Celebrate elders' diversity in social organizations and agencies.
- Training and Education:
  - Offer LGTB-specific curriculum in university and college settings.
  - Make available training sessions for professionals working in health care systems, social services agencies, and homecare services.
  - Educate social groups and organizations of LTGTB elders' needs.
  - Train providers to understand, follow, or challenge current policies and legislation on temporary or alternate decision makers in their regions.

- Outreach:
  - Develop sensitive outreach programs to older adults and their families with specific emphasis on multiply marginalized populations such as First Nations, poor, ethnic, racial, and sexual minorities.
- Policy:
  - Create options inside gay/lesbian and mainstream sectors.
  - Create opportunities for dialogue between sectors.
  - Review and revise all organizational/agency policies for LGTB visibility and inclusion.
  - Develop a diversity policy.
  - Ensure visibility of sexual orientation and gender identity in diversity policy.
  - Lobby for increased funding for programs.
- Practice:
  - Create environments of recognition and support.
    - Use appropriate language.
    - Adapt assessments—ask the right questions.
    - Use inclusive written materials and images.
    - Incorporate LGTB celebration, topics, and symbols.
  - Talk about sexuality.
  - Include families of choice in decision making.
  - Recognize complex psychosocial issues.
    - Identity: coming out, self-identification, identification with community
    - Vulnerability: impact of lifelong exposure to stigma
    - Isolation: managing stigma, exposure to discrimination (Brotman et al., 2006b, p. 11)

Conclusion

> While currently, there are not many visible LGTB people accessing services, it is important to be prepared for the future. There are many more vocal older adults who will expect to be welcomed and will demand change if it has not already happened (64-year-old lesbian).

Times continue to change. The majority of legislation bringing equality to LGTB people has come into effect. There is still much social change that is required. It is not enough any more to say, "We don't discriminate. We don't refuse anyone service." Or "We don't have any LGTB people in our facility." Being pro-active about creating visibility and welcome will prove beneficial rather than having to scramble when challenged!

References

Ambrose, M., January 21, 2006. Retiring back into the closet. Globe and Mail 12, F7.
Brotman, S., Ryan, B., Cormier, R., 2003. The health and social service needs of gay and lesbian elders and their families in Canada. Gerontologist 43 (2), 192–202.

Brotman, S., Ryan, B., Meyer, L., 2006a. The Health and Social Service Needs of Gay and Lesbian Elders. Final Report. McGill University School of Social Work, Montreal, QC.

Brotman, S., Ryan, B., Meyer, L., 2006b. The Health and Social Service Needs of Gay and Lesbian Seniors and Their Families in Canada. Executive Summary and Training Materials. McGill University School of Social Work, Montreal, QC.

Fritsch, T., 2005. HIV/AIDS and the older adult: an exploratory study of age-related differences in access to medical and social services. J. Appl. Gerontol. 24 (1), 35–54.

glbtq encyclopedia of gay, lesbian, bisexual, transgender & queer culture. <http://www.glbtq.com/>

Holland, C.A., Rabbitt, P.M.A., 1991. Ageing memory: use versus impairment. Br. J. Psychol. 82, 29–38.

Réseau des LESBIENNES du Québec. Retrieved September 15, 2009. <http://www.rlq-qln.algi.qc.ca/ainee_en.html/>

Riddle, D.I., 1985. Riddle homophobic scale. <http://www2.hawaii.edu/~lgbti/Attitudes%20Toward%20Difference%20Survey%20%20%20The%20Riddle%20Scale.pdf>

Spitzer, R.L., 1981. The diagnostic status of homosexuality in DSM-III: a reformulation of the issues. Am. J. Psychiatry 138, 210–215.

5 Union perspectives on abuse prevention in long-term care: current situation, future possibilities

Marcy Cohen

Unions, representing the staff in long-term care facilities, can and often do play a critical role in preventing abuse of long-term care residents. And yet, the contribution unions make to abuse prevention is often overlooked. This is due, in large measure, to the fact that unions have a legal obligation to represent their members if accused of resident abuse. As a result, they are often viewed in oppositional terms by the facility, resident, and/or the resident's family when an abuse issue is investigated.

This chapter analyzes the role of unions in abuse prevention at the individual, facility, and systems levels, and suggests that unions have a significant contribution to make in abuse prevention by ensuring due process, encouraging their members to report abuse, and most importantly, in developing strategies in coalition with community groups for addressing systemic abuse at the facility and system levels.

This discussion focuses specifically on the Hospital Employees' Union (HEU), the union that represents the majority of the direct and indirect care staff working in British Columbia's (BC) licensed long-term care facilities. In considering both future and current roles of the union, academic literature is reviewed as well as the practices and policies in BC and other jurisdictions to reduce the incidence of resident abuse. Also, a number of suggestions are presented on how the HEU and other health care unions in BC and elsewhere could work more closely with residents, families, and community groups in reducing resident abuse.

For the purposes of this chapter, the definition of resident abuse includes "sexual, financial, emotional, and physical abuse" and "neglect" as defined in the Adult Care regulations of the Community Care and Assisted Living Act (2004). It is, at the same time, also important to note that abuse occurs on a continuum:

> *There are both different types of abuse or neglect and different levels of harm that can occur. The actions may range from the cumulative effect of "little indignities," that erode personal dignity and feelings of security, to gross neglect and malicious assaults.*
>
> Spencer (2002, p. 2)

Union context and history

The HEU represents more than 80% of the staff working in most of BC's licensed residential care facilities—licensed practical nurses, resident care attendants, activity workers, rehabilitation assistants, dietary staff, and house-keeping staff—everyone other than registered nurses and rehabilitation/recrea-tion therapists. The union's role in preventing resident abuse in long-term care dates back to the 1970s when HEU first organized the staff in the private nurs-ing home sector in BC.

During that organizing drive, the union highlighted issues of resident neglect and low staffing levels, linking poor working conditions for staff with poor car-ing conditions for residents (Webb, 1994). The success of this organizing drive and public support for the union's linking of caring and working conditions were critical in pushing the provincial government, in the late 1970s, to establish a legislative and funding framework that would improve quality standards in BC's long-term care sector (Webb, 1994). This included the passage of the 1978 Long-Term Care Act, the development of funding guidelines for staffing (i.e., the Ministry of Health 1979 *Staffing Funding Guidelines*), and the provisions of financial and expert assistance to support not-for-profit community organiza-tions in building long-term care residential facilities (Ostry, 2006).

Over the years, the union has continued to advocate for improved work-ing and caring conditions. In 2001, based on growing concerns from members working in long-term care about their capacity to provide appropriate and compassionate care to residents with rising levels of acuity, the union made increased staffing levels a priority bargaining issue. The union worked in coali-tion with community and seniors groups in advocating for better staffing levels and negotiated an agreement with the provincial government to add 300 new care aide positions in long-term care.

Since May 2001, the union has been on the defensive with the closure of many long-term care facilities, the shift from not-for-profit to for-profit deliv-ery, and the contracting out of health support positions (i.e., cleaning, laundry, and food services). As a consequence, the union has not been in a position to advocate for improvements in care standards, and, in many cases, front-line staff report that working and caring conditions have deteriorated with the increase in the complexity of residents and no equivalent rise in staffing levels or training standards.

The context, however, has begun to shift once again. The combination of signing a new, four-year collective agreement that provides more stability in the sector, and the growing concerns from long-term care administrators, resi-dents, and families regarding quality of care have created new opportunities to address issues of substandard care, abuse, and neglect.

In the fall of 2006, a new multi-stakeholder, provincial-level Residential Care Policy Committee was formed—with representation from the Ministry of Health, health employers, unions, and physicians. Its mandate is to exam-ine training standards, staffing, and quality care issues in BC's long-term and assisted living facilities. HEU and the other unions in the Facilities Bargaining Association advocated for this Committee during the 2006 round of bargaining as part of policy discussions with the Ministry of Health and the health authorities.

Further discussion on the relationship between union strategies for improving the quality of care, staffing levels and training standards, and abuse prevention are provided in the sections that follow. This chapter looks at the individual, facility, and system level factors that must be addressed in tackling abuse, and proposes a number of abuse-prevention strategies.

Individual level factors: the union role

It is the responsibility of the servicing representative, working with union locals at the work site, to represent any worker accused of abuse. This duty to represent is a legal obligation for unions, not dissimilar to the requirement of legal representation in the criminal justice system. It is intended to ensure due process and fair treatment when a worker is accused of a serious infraction that could result in discipline or termination. In BC, when a member is accused of abuse, he or she is sent home while management conducts an investigation and decides on a course of action. Little is known, however, about the prevalence, types of abuse, or results of abuse-related investigations because there are no requirements to collect statistical information either provincially or nationally (Spencer, 2002).

In an informal survey of HEU servicing representatives, it was clear that HEU members have been fired based on evidence that they were unsuitable to work with the elderly, but this is a relatively infrequent occurrence. There are many less clear-cut cases, where staff burnout is a contributing factor, and others where the individual reports that he or she has "hit out" at a resident (based on duty-to-report files). In these cases, there has been considerable variation in how the situations have been handled. Numerous servicing representatives expressed concern about management's capacity and willingness to address issues of staff burnout and to conduct investigations in ways that take into account institution-level, contributing factors (i.e., staff burnout, staff shortages, lack of supervision, overtime rates, etc.).

Many of the individual risk factors associated with the likelihood that an individual staff member will abuse a resident—burnout, substance abuse, depression, and family or personal problems (Hawes, 2002)—suggest that early identification and interventions are critical and are best achieved if the union and management staff are appropriately trained, supported, and encouraged to work in conjunction with residents and their families. In a report of a non-random survey of 718 community nurses in England, Manthorpe et al. (2005) note that "almost all respondents said that further training would be beneficial, indicating a lack of professional self-confidence in dealing with possible abusive situations" (p. 24). Kozak and Lukawiecki (2001) point to the importance of employing an independent ombudsman who can monitor the facility and act as an advocate both for frail older adults and staff.

There is a requirement in BC's Community Care and Assisted Living Act (2004) for front-line staff to report abuse if and when it occurs, and staff can be disciplined for failure to do so. To meet this obligation, staff must have the knowledge and skills to both identify different forms of abuse and to, ideally, prevent abuse from occurring in the first place. In BC's public college programs for residential care attendants (RCAs) and licensed practical nurses (LPNs), the curriculum includes education on abuse prevention and the duty to report any incidence of abuse (Dixon, 2006, personal communication). The public colleges also play a role in screening out workers who are unsuitable to work with the elderly (Dixon, 2006, personal communication). There is, however, little regulation of private college training programs or curriculum in BC. As a result, it is uncertain how and to what extent abuse prevention education and screening of students for appropriateness is part of the private training system.

In terms of staff disclosures some, but certainly not all, of the servicing representatives, report that they remind members of their duty to report incidents of abuse. They also note that many facilities provide in-service education on how to manage care and diffuse aggressive behavior in residents who suffer from dementia. This type of education is an important abuse-prevention strategy that should be regularly provided and mandated by government.

In summary, there is a need for a number of important initiatives at the provincial level. In particular, increased training and ongoing support for union and management staff is needed to develop and implement abuse-prevention strategies and to respond appropriately when resident abuse occurs. Increased opportunities for dialogue between union and management staff and residents and their families should be mandated by government as an essential component of all abuse-prevention initiatives. There is also a need for provincial action to ensure that there is appropriate curriculum and screening of students in private as well as public RCA and LPN training programs. Further, there is a need for an independent ombudsman with a specific mandate to monitor facilities, conduct abuse investigations, and advocate on behalf of both staff and residents.

Facility- and system-level issues

Layered over the individual risk factors are the systemic issues. Reducing the likelihood that an individual resident will be abused cannot be achieved simply by weeding out the "inappropriate" workers. System-wide issues and, in particular, funding levels for direct care staff and staff training are identified as of paramount importance in the literature on abuse prevention. As Professor Catherine Hawes (2002) states in her testimony before the US Senate Committee on Finance "there is a remarkable consensus across diverse studies and surveys of stakeholders"[1] as to the causes and factors that contribute to abuse and neglect in nursing homes. They are:

- Staffing shortages that cause neglect and create stressful working conditions in which abuse is more likely to occur
- Staff burnout, often a product of staffing shortages, mandatory overtime, and the fact that many staff must work two jobs to survive financially
- Poor staff training, particularly on the impact of dementia and how to interpret and manage challenging behaviors among residents (Hawes, 2002, p. 7)

Similar issues were identified in two Health Canada projects conducted in the late 1990s on abuse prevention in long-term care (Kozak and Lukawiecki, 2001). The researchers report that in every province, long-term care residents, staff (both clinical and administrative), volunteers, and family members raised concerns about the reduction in direct care staffing:

Health care workers, families, and residents expressed increasing anger at the continuing decline in appropriate care funding and their frustration at being unable to affect changes or have an impact on policy development.
Kozak and Lukawiecki (2001, p. 12)

These conclusions were supported in the 2006 Canadian study, *A way forward: Abuse prevention in institutional settings* (Spencer et al., 2008). The study links the increased risk of abuse and neglect with the growing "care gap" in Canadian long-term care facilities:

According to the stakeholders, the average care needs of residents across the range of care facilities have become heavier and significantly more complex over the past 15 years.... Levels of staffing, along with qualifications, training, and supervision of persons who provide the care has not kept pace and, in many cases, has decreased.
Spencer et al. (2008, p. 44)

A factor—other than appropriate staffing levels and training—repeatedly highlighted in the literature as important in addressing issues of abuse and neglect is a "supportive and respectful environment" (Kozak and Lukawiecki, 2001). As Pring (2005), a researcher from the United Kingdom, noted, a lack of attention to organization culture and professional inaction are key in hiding facility level systemic abuse. This is certainly the experience in some facilities in BC, where abuse has been repeatedly reported by HEU members and staff (Summerland General Hospital, 2001), but action to address these issues was very slow in coming.

The Health Canada report, *Stand By Me* (Kozak and Lukawiecki, 2001), makes a somewhat similar, but more general, point:

The first step in prevention is acknowledging that abuse and neglect are occurring. The attitude still prevails that abuse does not happen in "our facility," even though participants across the country indicated that abuse and neglect is a regular feature of LTC (especially the more subtle forms of psychological abuse).

Kozak and Lukawiecki (2001, p. 15)

The "normalization" of abuse in long-term care was raised by HEU's RCAs and LPNs in focus groups organized during the 2005 consultations on BC's *Community Care and Assisted Living* regulations (Cohen, 2005). The care aides and LPNs in the focus groups indicated how low staffing levels meant that they lacked the time to talk with, turn or mobilize residents, provide extra assistance with eating, or ensure that they were regularly taking fluids. As a result, residents were more likely to feel isolated, get bed sores, be malnourished, and suffer from dehydration. In addition, diapers are increasingly being used as an alternative to toileting because it saves staff time. And yet, this is very humiliating for residents, particularly given the rules restricting how often staff are allowed to change the residents' diapers. Staff also reported that residents who were isolated and without a family member to advocate on their behalf were most likely to experience neglect. As their care providers, front-line staff were often the residents' only advocate or support.

Facility-level actions

Based on the research evidence, it is clear that strategies on abuse prevention and improving the quality of service in long-term care settings are intricately linked. A study conducted jointly by BC's Occupational Health and Safety Agency for Healthcare, University of British Columbia researchers, and HEU (Yassi et al., 2004) points to some of the ways that facilities can reduce the risk of patient abuse. Although the study was not designed to look specifically at this issue—but rather at the relationship among staff injury rates, staffing levels, and organizational culture—it does provide some very important insights into facility-level factors that contribute to improved quality care and abuse prevention.

Key findings include:

* Although the facilities in the study received similar levels of funding from the Ministry of Health, they differed in funding proportions allocated to front-line staff positions.
* Facilities with higher front-line staffing were perceived by care staff to be doing a better job in providing good quality care under difficult circumstances.
* Facilities with higher front-line staffing levels were more likely to have an organizational culture that supported quality care, including an engaged environment, a substantive philosophy of care, and policy and procedures to support this philosophy.

The three organizational culture factors identified through this study as important to improving the working and caring conditions are also important in reducing the incidence of resident abuse. The first factor, an engaged environment, supports early identification of problems, ongoing learning, and flexible delivery of care to support resident needs. While most of the facilities in the study had staff meetings, at some facilities, staff members were encouraged to speak up and provide input, while other facility meetings were a formality with little opportunity for genuine staff input. There were also differences in the extent to which supervisors and managers had an "open door policy" and were, therefore, willing to meet with individual care staff on an informal basis. As a result, staff had very different experiences in terms of their ability to influence their residents' care and raise concerns with their supervisors or managers.

The second significant organizational factor was the extent to which a facility had a substantive philosophy of care. While all the facilities in the study claimed to be promoting quality care, there were significant differences between facilities in the information they provided staff on the health conditions of residents and the extent to which care aides were involved in care planning meetings. If staff members are regularly updated on their residents' physical and emotional health status, they will be better equipped to respond appropriately to their needs and avoid situations where abuse might occur.

And the third factor influencing the quality of the work environment was concrete policies and practices. This includes policies for addressing issues such as resident aggression. Staff in all of the facilities in the study reported that responding to aggressive residents with dementia was part of their job. Significant differences, however, emerged among facilities that had concrete policies and processes in place to follow up and support staff after an incident of resident aggression had occurred.

Taken together, these organizational characteristics—an engaged environment, a substantive philosophy of care, and concrete policies and practices—encourage staff to provide a high standard of care, and at the same time, identify problems before there is a crisis or negative incident. It is important to re-emphasize that the facilities in the study, which had a positive work culture, were the same facilities with higher front-line staffing levels. While this research did not compare for-profit and not-for-profit facilities, there is BC research from 2001, as well as research from other jurisdictions, comparing staffing levels in not-for-profit and for-profit long-term care facilities (McGregor et al., 2005). The BC research shows that not-for-profit facilities have higher front-line staffing levels despite the fact that both for-profit and not-for-profit facilities received the same level of funding from the Ministry of Health.

Quite clearly, facility-level abuse-prevention strategies require provincial level action to mandate adequate government funding for care staff, provincial regulations to ensure these resources are actually directed to front-line staff, and consistent policies to encourage a respectful and supportive environment. On this latter point, a quote from the Canadian Network for the Prevention of Elder Abuse website provides a good summary of the discussion in this section:

An abuse-free environment is seldom created by simply having a non-abuse policy. It is created by developing an entire living environment that is supportive of the rights of residents, promotes quality of care, and addresses the

residents' needs. It is also created by having a positive working environ-
ment for people who work there, so they can provide the needed care and
assistance.

                                                            CNPEA (undated, p. 16)

System-level actions

As noted in the previous section, many of the abuse-prevention measures
discussed in this chapter—appropriate staffing levels, organizational initiatives to promote greater collaboration and input from staff and residents on
care-related issues, abuse-prevention policies, training programs, and an independent ombudsman to conduct abuse investigations—require action at the
provincial and/or federal level. This section focuses on two of the key mechanisms that can make a difference in tackling abuse—mandated advocacy programs, and effective oversight and enforcement of licensing requirements in
residential care.

In terms of a mandated advocacy program, there are some very positive examples from the United States. Since the 1970s, there has been a very strong national
consumer movement advocating for residents and staff in long-term care, led
by the National Citizens' Coalition for Nursing Home Reform (NCCNHR)
(http://www.nccnhr.org). This organization was established because of the widely
reported problems of abuse, neglect, and substandard care in America's primarily
private long-term care sector. As a result of advocacy from organizations such
as NCCNHR, the US government passed the Older Americans Act in 1981 that
mandated, among other things, a Long-Term Care Ombudsman program. This
program is funded federally and operates in every state. The program provides a
coordinated approach to advocacy, including a network of locally trained volunteers, who advocate on behalf of individual residents; and professional staff at the
state level, who provide systematic advocacy to the entire sector, including representation at the state legislatures (Spencer, 2006).

There is no equivalent in Canada. In BC, as in other provinces, there are
a number of volunteer organizations, including Advocates for Care Reform,
the BC Centre for Elder Advocacy and Support, and the Seniors Advocacy
Network, who advocate on behalf of vulnerable seniors, but there is no federal or provincial legislative mandate or ongoing funding to support their
work. In BC, the Seniors Advocacy Network recently gained support from the
Federation of Canadian Municipalities for establishing regional seniors' advocacy offices funded by the provincial and federal governments.

In 2004, a report from the Ontario Ministry of Health's Long-Term Care
Division, suggested that a long-term care ombudsman be established in Ontario
to serve as an independent advocate for seniors in long-term care, but this
has yet to happen. It is also interesting to note that while a number of provinces have ombudsman programs that act as "watch dogs" for public services,

only Nova Scotia "has staff in their Office of the Ombudsman whose work is focused specifically on seniors in long-term care" (Spencer, 2006, p. 33). Additional support for a seniors and/or long-term care ombudsman program from the federal and/or provincial governments in Canada would go a long way in tackling the issue of abuse, neglect, and substandard care in long-term care.

It is interesting to note that changes in licensing regulations and enforcement in recent years in both Ontario and Alberta have occurred as a result of extensive media coverage regarding the substandard care, abuse, and neglect in their long-term care facilities. In response to negative media publicity in Ontario in 2004, the Ministry of Health increased funding for care staff, introduced surprise inspections, and a website http://www.health.gov.on.ca/english/public/ program/ltc/15_facilities.html where the public can access information on the findings of inspection reports and verified concerns at individual facilities. And in late 2006, they are expected to further tighten their licensing rules to include mandatory family councils, higher penalties for facilities that fail to comply with licensing findings, whistle-blower protection for staff and residents, 24-hour nursing coverage, a minimum of two baths a week, and a *Resident Bill of Rights* (Talaga, 2006).

In Alberta, the government response to similar negative publicity and an Auditor-General's report that found substandard care in one-third of the 25 facilities reviewed has been slower in coming (Baxter, 2006).[2] The government has announced $42 million next year for increased care staff, but critics argue that will still not bring Alberta's long-term care facilities up to the promised 3.6 hours of care per day. Additional requirements for staff training, criminal record checks, and abuse-prevention polices are expected to be introduced in Alberta next year.

In terms of the BC licensing regime for residential care, there are some very positive features of the Community Care and Assisted Living Act and regulations, including an inclusive definition of abuse, whistle-blower protection for staff and residents, mandatory reporting of abuse, and mandated abuse-prevention policies. There are, at the same time, some very glaring weaknesses. There are no minimum staffing levels or training requirements, no definition of what should be included in abuse-prevention policies, and no public reporting on licensing violations and substantiated complaints. The Ministry of Health's funding formula for long-term care has not been updated since 1979, and access to information on results of complaints investigations and inspections can only be obtained through a Freedom of Information request. There is, in addition, no requirement or dedicated funding for facilities to establish independent family councils and considerable variation among the health authorities in terms of how they implement provincial regulations. These issues require immediate attention to ensure that BC's licensing rules and enforcement mechanisms for long-term care are, in fact, protecting residents from abuse, neglect, and substandard care.

Conclusion

From this discussion of the factors that contribute to resident abuse and measures required to reduce incidence of abuse, it is clear that despite some differences in perspective among unions, seniors advocates, health care professionals, residents, and their families, there are many common concerns and opportunities for collaboration. By working together to develop and advocate for improvements in quality of care and abuse prevention, we will all be more effective in achieving our goals.

References

Baxter, J., May 4, 2006. Province toughens nursing home rules. Edmonton J. B5.

Canadian Network for the Prevention of Elder Abuse (undated). Abuse in institutions: FAQs about abuse in institutions. <Retrieved from http://www.cnpea.ca/abuse_in_institutions.pdf 25.07.08>

Cohen, M., 2005. Notes from focus groups organized by the Licensing Branch of Ministry of Health with approximate 25 HEU Care Aides and LPNs, January 25, 2005 (Vancouver) and January 26, 2005 (Victoria).

Community Care and Assisted Act, 2004. Adult Care Regulations: 119/99 section 4 and 5; Appendix 1, 217/2004 section 12(d) and section 13; Schedule 1, 457/2004, section 6.

Hawes, C., 2002. Elder abuse in residential long-term care facilities: what is known about prevalence, causes and prevention. Testimony before the US Senate Committee on Finance, p. 7.

Kozak, J., Lukawiecki, T., 2001. Stand By Me: Preventing Abuse and Neglect of Residents in Long-Term Care Settings. Health Canada, Ottawa, ON.

McGregor, M.J., Cohen, M., McGrail, K., Boemeling, A.M., Adler, R., Schulzer, M., 2005. Differences in staffing levels in British Columbia's funded long-term care facilities by ownership type (not-for-profit vs. for-profit). Can. Med. Assoc. J. 172 (1), 637–641.

Manthorpe, J., Perkins, N., Penhale, B., Pinkney, L., Kingsley, P., 2005. Select questions: considering the issues raised by a parliamentary select committee inquiry into elder abuse. J. Adult. Prot. 7 (3), 24.

Ostry, A., 2006. Change and Continuity in Canada's Health Care System. CHA Press, Ottawa, ON.

Pring, J., 2005. Why did it take so long to expose the abusive regime at Longcare. J. Adult. Prot. 7 (1), 15–23.

Spencer, C., Charpentier, M., McDonald, L., Beaulieu, M., Harbison, J., Hirst, S., Podnieks, E., 2008. National snapshot: preventing abuse and neglect of older adults in institutions. Prepared for the "A Way Forward Project: Promising Approaches to Abuse Prevention in Institutional Settings". <http://www.elderabuse.aging.utoronto.ca/files/National%20Snapshot%20-%20Full%20Report.pdf>

Spencer, C., 2002. Is what we have in Canada working? A look at the use of special legislation to protect older persons in care from abuse and neglect. Paper presented at the Annual Meeting of the Canadian Association on Gerontology, Montreal, Quebec.

Spencer, C., 2006. A way forward: abuse prevention in institutional settings: highlights from the national snapshot. Power point presentation.

Summerland General Hospital, August 28, 2001. Minutes of the Summerland General Hospital and Extended Care Special Labour Management Meeting. [These minutes document complaints of reported incidence of abuse from HEU members from 1993 to 2000.]

Talaga, T., October 3, 2006. Nursing home face tougher rules. Toronto Star.

Webb, P., 1994. Heart of Health Care: The First 50 Years. Hospital Employees Union, Vancouver, BC, pp. 39–47.

Yassi, A., Cohen, M., Cvitkovich, Y., Park, I., Ratner, P.A., Ostry, A.S., Village, J., Pollak, N., 2004. Factors associated with staff injuries in intermediate care facilities in British Columbia, Canada. Nurs. Res. 53 (2), 1–12.

6 Abuse of older adults: an Ontario criminal justice perspective

Patricia Fleischmann

Although elder abuse has been acknowledged as a social problem for many years by individuals from a number of disciplines, the concept is relatively new in the criminal justice sector. When compared to child abuse or domestic violence, elder abuse cases have not attained the same attention, energy, or commitment. A groundswell of advocacy and forward thinking, however, is providing constructive change within police agencies. This encouraging support has been demonstrated through the implementation of administrative procedures and policies, the development of specialized positions or units, and educational efforts. While these reforms are far from complete, determined and dedicated individuals throughout criminal justice organizations are championing for the safety and well-being of older persons, for their right to live free of abuse and violence, and for their right to self-determination.

Framing the problem

Any discussion of elder abuse must be framed within the context of an aging population. The worldwide increase in the number of older persons is having and will continue to have global ramifications for governments, social service agencies, medical and health care practitioners, science and technology, the housing industry, transportation providers, and the for-profit sector, to name but a few. The United Nations General Assembly (1992) notes in its *Proclamation on Ageing*:

> ... that the ageing of the world's population represents an unparalleled, but urgent, policy and programme challenge to Governments, non-governmental organizations, and private groups to ensure that the needs of the aged and their human resource potential are adequately addressed.
>
> United Nations (1992, p. 1)

The United Nations (1991) has also declared the following as principles for the worlds' older persons: independence, participation, care, self-fulfillment, and dignity. These principles communicate the message of safe environments, access to legal services, autonomy, care and protection, and living in dignity and with security, while being free from physical abuse, mental abuse, or exploitation. Canada has similar but distinct principles on aging: that all citizens have the right to dignity, independence, participation, fairness, and security (see *National Framework on Aging*, Health Canada, 1998).

Both the Canadian and Ontario governments recognize that seniors are impacted by crime. Although the prevalence of the fear of crime is described as being greater than actual crimes against seniors (Cohen, 2001; Novak and Campbell, 2001), elder abuse is reputed to be considerably under-reported (Bond et al., 1999; Podnieks et al., 1990; Statistics Canada, 2001; Trevitt and Gallagher, 1996). Indisputably, the criminal justice system will be tested in its recognition of and response to elder abuse given the changing demographics. This chapter, which developed from an informal survey of law enforcement and provincial government personnel and civil litigators, provides a broad overview of what is currently transpiring among Ontario's criminal justice practitioners.

Definitions and terminology

As noted elsewhere in this volume, the lack of consensus around definitions and terminology is problematic for the study of older adult abuse. Within Canada, several definitions are used. Health Canada, for example, has adopted the WHO/INPEA (2002) definition, which explains that elder abuse is "a single or repeated act, or lack of appropriate action occurring in any relationship where there is an expectation of trust that causes harm or distress to an older person" (p. 3). The Province of Ontario (2008) employs a broader interpretation of elder abuse defining it as "any act or omission that harms a senior or jeopardizes his or her health or welfare" while Procedure 05-22, Abuse of Elderly or Vulnerable Persons (Toronto Police Service, 2000), which directs officers' actions, states that elder abuse is "harm (financial, psychological, physical, including sexual, neglect, or any combination thereof) caused to a person over the age of 65 years by a person in a position of trust or authority" (p. 2). This particular definition of elder abuse does not include stranger crimes, such as the scams or cons perpetrated against older adults; these are investigated by the Toronto Police Service Fraud Unit—Project Senior Section. The Service further recognizes that older adult abuse may not always be criminal in nature, yet its impact can be both profound and debilitating to a senior.

Financial abuse of older adults

Financial abuse is one type of abuse that may be experienced by an older adult, often in conjunction with psychological abuse. By and large, law enforcement personnel will acknowledge that financial abuse is the offence most commonly disclosed by older victims, as well as by concerned family members, friends, and service providers. Police receive the most requests for assistance for this offence. Specialized investigative units will confirm the high proportion of occurrences that involve financial abuse: from thefts to frauds and various other criminal offences by family members, friends, professionals, care providers, and substitute decision makers. Although older adults may be willing to discuss their financial victimization, it does not necessarily translate to an actual police report. Many older adults will minimize, rationalize, and even deny the existence of these abusive relationships. These same victims are often reluctant to have the suspect, someone they have an established relationship with and usually a family member, be held accountable for their actions. This is a situation police encounter on a frequent basis, with considerable frustration in their attempt to aid older adult victims of financial crime. It is particularly disheartening for officers encountering such reluctance to report by those emotionally devastated by their losses, near impoverishment, or even homeless as a result.

How can the justice system better respond to such a situation? What recommendations can criminal justice practitioners provide?

With this type of crime, financial institutions play a major role. It is paramount for law enforcement and the financial sector to work collaboratively with one another. Having a solid connection with both the corporate office and local branches allows for ease of communication and increased cooperation throughout the investigative process. Police services must actively encourage both leadership and advocacy from within. Employees in this sector cannot and must not be allowed to believe that suspect behavior or criminal action that victimizes their clients is not their concern. Nor can corporate protocols condone this behavior. All financial institutions must train and inform their personnel, from senior management through to staff at the branch level, of the warning signs of financial abuse and just as importantly, ensure that it is not systemically ignored. Additionally, these actions need to be carefully and thoroughly documented. More critically still, financial abuse, suspected or otherwise, must also be acted upon whether or not it meets the threshold of a criminal offence. Not only is this responsible citizenship, it is astute business practice. Commonly, the relationship between banks and their customers is one of debtor and creditor. That is, in the course of normal financial transactions, a fiduciary relationship does not exist. Although there is no law that places a fiduciary duty on financial institutions in such cases, many would argue that this needs to happen. There is, however, case law that supports the position of a fiduciary duty to clients in certain circumstances. Will the Courts, however, impose this fiduciary responsibility if the bank has offered financial advice to a customer? If nothing else, it is a moral obligation owed to their clients. Civil liability is also an avenue that can be explored by interested parties, if financial victimization occurs.

The Canadian Bankers Association notes in a 2006 publication that their member banks engage in "… employee training and rigorous internal procedures, customer awareness programs, and cooperation with governments, law enforcement agencies, and other bodies at both the national and international levels" in the effort to avert financial crimes (p. 8). The Canadian Bankers Association does not, however, have a protocol for their members to follow in cases of elder abuse by persons in positions of trust or authority. A specific financial abuse policy, if not already in place, should be developed at the corporate level and widely communicated to both personnel and clients.

Financial institutions are known to hold information sessions or customer awareness programs. Through these, supplemented with supportive literature, older clients, along with family members, friends, substitute decision makers, or advocates can learn about typical profiles of victims and abusers, common indicators of this type of crime, available assistance, and, most importantly, how to get help. All financial institutions have corporate publications. These corporate newsletters can explain in clear, succinct, and straightforward language, the common indicators of financial abuse, as well as the institution's position on this crime. Additionally, for Internet-savvy clients, relevant information should be posted on appropriate banking websites. Just as importantly, though, is a user-friendly website to enable a person to quickly navigate and locate the applicable information.

The Canadian Bankers Association (2007) also states that banks continue to fulfill their obligation to "… act on their suspicion and report the suspected abuse to another family member or the authorities" (p. 8). Sections within the Personal Information Protection and Electronic Documents Act (Department of Justice Canada, 2006), however, can cause difficulties with the sharing of information, and the Association is promoting changes to the Act that would allow for disclosure of personal information when it would clearly be in the best interest of the person or for the broader public good.

Associated arms of the banking sector are trust companies. These distinct financial entities offer a wide variety of services to their clients. Services such as will and estate planning, estate and trust management, even acting as guardians or Power of Attorney for property for capable persons, or providing custodial services for an incapable person's property provide a viable option for the individual. They may offer choices such as alter-ego (individual) or joint-partner services that provide safer, more protective alternatives than the usual joint bank account option. Still, banks and trust companies need to communicate more effectively with one another so that each knows what the other can supply in the way of customer service, thus enhancing their clients' financial security. Most likely, law enforcement is not aware of these services, but after this becomes common knowledge, there should be improved advocacy and support for joint initiatives that serve the interests of the institution and the client. This venture supports not only the mission and vision statements but also the core values of police services with community safety and community partnerships being a strong tenant throughout.

Outside of the financial sector, the Financial Consumer Agency of Canada offers Canadians several such publications in the form of tip sheets. Likewise, the Financial Services Commission of Ontario has appropriate information listed and even provides links to other provincial and federal governmental departments and various international resources. Links can be made to local police services, if not already established, to service providers and other organizations, furthering these important messages. Specialized police officers can serve as regular feature writers or guest presenters and should be encouraged to do so.

How should customer service staff, financial planners, or managers act in situations where they suspect financial abuse?

Staff must speak directly to and privately with the older adult. That is, the conversation must be held without the suspected abuser present. Then, without being paternalistic or patronizing, questions can be raised about unusual activity in their accounts, such as uncharacteristic checks, atypical cash transactions, aberrant patterns of financial behaviour, unpaid bills, bank statements or cheques being sent to a different address, the unexplained or sudden interest of another person in the senior's life, and the potential negative implications of such actions. The older adult can be informed that the bank's associated trust company can be contacted for additional options. If trust companies take on a custodial role, albeit at a cost, the older client may avoid potential or further problems with persons taking advantage of them, thereby decreasing the risk of abuse.

It becomes decidedly more complex when suspected financial abuse is occurring in cases where the victim is not considered capable or where there is a substitute decision maker acting on behalf of the older adult. This is likely a matter for both the local law enforcement agency, as it falls under the *Criminal Code of Canada*, and local guardianship investigators. In the Province of Ontario, it is the Office of the Public Guardian and Trustee that would engage in such investigations, if it meets the criteria established in the Substitute Decisions Act of 1992. In the Toronto area, the Advocacy Centre for the Elderly, a community legal aid clinic serving older adults, has been of tremendous assistance to law enforcement in such criminal cases, including those where capacity is an issue.

What about privacy concerns?

There is considerable debate around confidentiality. Employees should ask permission by making a direct enquiry such as, "May I call the police?" If an affirmative answer is given, then police should be immediately contacted. Arrangements can then be made for any necessary assistance to the client, through the institution or the local police. Moreover, if an employee makes a direct observation, that is, she or he is a witness to a financial abuse event, a call to police is appropriate. This action does not breach confidentiality policies and provides clients with a much needed and often neglected criminal justice option.

There are two circumstances where agencies may breach confidentiality: when business records are subject to judicial authorization and when the older adult is in a state of imminent harm or will cause harm to another person. An employee does not need permission from management, nor should management be the first phone call placed when an older adult is in this situation. Police must be the first call made, and if the circumstances warrant, it should be a 9-1-1 emergency call. After police have been contacted, a call to management can follow.

From a criminal justice perspective, police agencies should contemplate putting institutions on notice if they are conducting investigations of financial abuse, where an elderly client has been or is being victimized. Banks, as commercial entities, have no wish to be held liable for monies lost to unscrupulous cons or to be considered financially complicit in such matters, if no action is taken to protect client assets. They will take immediate steps to safeguard their interests and those of their clients upon notification. If police agencies decide to provide written notice, which holds more weight than an oral notification, their respective legal and corporate units should be rigorously consulted for advice.

Local law enforcement as a resource

Police, in specialized positions or units, are a commonly underused source for information. In the Toronto Police Service, for example, some of the duties of the officer responsible for Vulnerable Persons Issues include acting as a community referral resource, liaising with community service agencies and groups to develop partnerships, supporting related community and Service functions, and facilitating as well as enhancing communications between community service providers and the Service. Specifically, these responsibilities speak to the Toronto Police Service's (2006a) *Vision Statement* and priorities of community partnerships, community safety and security, safety of vulnerable groups, as well as *delivery of service* (Toronto Police Service, 2006b).

Local neighborhood officers are another valuable and commonly underused resource. These officers can often be the best line of defence in a community because they know their neighbourhood: they know the residents, businesses, and criminals as well as the current levels and types of criminal activity. Communities at large, businesses, agencies, advocates, and individuals all can consult with these community officers, either on a formal or informal basis.

Communities with local elder abuse consultation teams should consider the inclusion of an individual with a law enforcement perspective to their membership. It is vital, though, to have the right fit: an officer who is familiar with the issues, someone in a specialized squad or in a dedicated role. Cases can be discussed and potential resolutions suggested, perhaps in ways never before considered, if the local police service is brought to the table. There are two basic options with consultation teams. With the senior victim's permission, specific details can be provided. Or, the case can be discussed in broad, non-specific terms, with the provision of the basic facts. There is a concern with this second option, however. Some argue it is an infringement on matters of privacy and confidentiality, particularly if multiple service providers are involved in the case. If, however, direct participation on a consultation team is not possible, police may be contacted for discussion of a specific issue on an as-needed basis.

What about legislation?

Unlike child abuse, there is no legal mandate to report elder abuse in Ontario. Neither is there specific adult protection legislation, although pertinent provincial statutes, such as the Substitute Decisions Act, 1992, do exist. Similarly, a charge of *elder abuse* does not exist under federal legislation, but certainly there are many sections in the *Criminal Code of Canada* that may pertain to elder abuse, depending upon the actual offence. Simply put, it is a matter of using the existing legislation appropriately. In Toronto and elsewhere throughout the province, the Advocacy Centre for the Elderly may be consulted for their expert legal assistance in such criminal investigations.

Current status of abuse and neglect cases in the criminal justice system: an Ontario perspective

Abuse and neglect of older adults is occurring in Toronto and around the province, as it is happening across the country and elsewhere. If Toronto is considered a reflection of what is taking place in other communities in the province, elder abuse is significantly under-reported. For example, a well-established local social service provider confidentially revealed in 2006 that fully 35% of the cliental of their agency reported living in abusive situations but had not disclosed the matter to police. This same manager revealed that the number, today, is closer to the 50% mark. Surveys of other social service agencies may very well yield similar data.

Some consider the criminal justice system to be ageist. Subtle and generally unrealized ageist behaviour can be detected in police personnel, prosecutors, defence counsel, and even the judiciary. It surfaces through interactions and the manner in which older adults are described, communicated with, and assumptions made. Unfortunately, it often emerges in the investigative stages among police personnel. A US study by Payne et al. (2001) sought to identify how police agencies responded to elder abuse allegations. Based on past experience, police respondents expected several obstacles would negatively impact their response to elder abuse. These obstacles included victims' fear of reporting, lack of police resources, failure of victims and witnesses to report, lack of personnel, delays in reporting, lack of cooperation from victims' families, witness/victim problems, and judicial obstacles. Police chiefs also reflected ageist beliefs and attitudes. Examples provided include: elderly victims aren't good witnesses; when an elderly victim is the sole witness and is considered senile, it is difficult to obtain a conviction without evidence of visible injuries; and an elderly victim is incapable of understanding or handling a criminal prosecution, which is typically a slow and cumbersome process.

The criminal justice system is also an adversarial process because it is offender-focused as opposed to being victim/complainant-centered. Simply being present in the courts is usually an uncomfortable experience for any victim, let alone an older victim of crime—someone who, likely, has never had interactions with the police before.

Although police today have a greater understanding of the issues surrounding elder abuse and are more adept at report-taking and appropriately categorizing elder abuse occurrences, this is not always the case. At present, no specialized course dealing with older adult abuse and neglect exists at the Ontario Police College (OPC), the provincial training facility for all police personnel in Ontario. There is, however, some good news. The OPC offers recruits a one-hour introduction to elder abuse in the domestic violence investigation course. Additionally, the fraud investigation course includes an elder abuse component, by way of a theft by power of attorney case example. It would be fair to say, then, that if elder abuse is under-reported as a crime, it also suffers from under-investigation.

Additionally, elder abuse cases are appreciably under-prosecuted. Very few actually make their way to the courts. Reasons may include lack of awareness on the part of crown attorneys of the issues, little or no training in working with older adults, unrealized ageist beliefs about elderly victims, or insufficient experience through limited opportunities for prosecution in such matters. Further, conclusions may be drawn that there is little chance for a successful prosecution in elder abuse cases. For example, in a late 1990s Toronto area case, the much younger wife of an older man suffering from dementia and other serious medical conditions was charged with failing to provide the necessaries of life and numerous property-related offences. The investigating officer thoroughly prepared the case for trial. It did not make it to trial, however, because of the assistant crown attorney's belief that there was no reasonable prospect for conviction. On the positive side, if such a case does make its way to criminal court, and there is a conviction of guilt, section 718.2 of the *Criminal Code of Canada* (Martin's Annual Criminal Code, 2006) states that the court shall also consider, for sentencing purposes, "… any relevant aggravating or mitigating circumstances relating to the offence or the offender …" and evidence where the offence was biased because of age or where the offender abused his or her position of trust or authority.

Specialized seniors' fraud units and S.C.A.T.

Progressive police agencies have specialized units where resources are directed at investigations of financial abuse of seniors. Toronto Police Service for example, has a Mass Marketing, Seniors, and Social Benefits Investigations section within its Fraud Unit. This section's mandate focuses on stranger-victim crimes such as boiler room operations, organized telemarketing schemes, social benefit frauds, and Internet frauds. Officers in the Project Senior subsection focus on major schemes centered on victimization of the elderly.

For several years now, Toronto Police Service has been an active member of S.C.A.T. (Senior Crimes Around Toronto). This is an informal criminal justice organization consisting of police and government personnel. The purpose of the group is to exchange information that may assist with criminal investigations pertaining to financial abuse of older adults by strangers. At the present time, there are nearly 30 members from eight police services in the Southern Ontario Golden Horseshoe Area and personnel from four government departments.

At the local level, divisional fraud investigators in Toronto, although not seniors' specialists, will undertake such cases as they arise. A number of other Services in Ontario have specialized units and dedicated investigators who deal with all aspects of older adult abuse. Over the past few years, case loads have risen substantially. Another police service, in a smaller community, has an officer working jointly with a social worker in a unique restorative justice program covering all types of abuse.

Police service standards and guidelines

The *Policing Standards Manual* (2000), section LE-021 "Elder and Vulnerable Adult Abuse," offers police service guidelines on elder abuse and vulnerable adult abuse. These include definitions, multidisciplinary coordination, and specifics for internal procedures. Many services approach this issue from a risk-management perspective and have tailored the guidelines to suit the needs of their respective agencies. Toronto Police Service has had an *Abuse of Elderly or Vulnerable Persons Procedure (05-22)* since 2000. This procedure directs officers' responses to these types of calls for service. Other police agencies have similar procedures in place.

Practice memorandum for crown attorneys

In Ontario, the *Crown Policy Manual* (2005) has the following major sections: Role of the Crown and the Crown Policy Manual; Professionalism, Independence and Accountability; Case Management; Victim Standards, and Practices; Fairness in Criminal Justice Process; Specific Types of Prosecutions; and lastly, Procedural Issues and Trial Practice. The Specific Types of Prosecutions section records 10 important categories but does not currently include elder abuse. According to Jacek (2006, personal communication), the Ministry of the Attorney General–Criminal Law Policy Branch considered and evaluated a practice memorandum on elder abuse for crown attorneys, although as of Fall 2009, it has not been implemented, nor at this time, is it expected to be implemented.

Multilanguage interpretation

Toronto is home to an estimated 75–150 languages; a City of Toronto report (2007) indicates that 47% of Toronto's population has a mother tongue other than Canada's two official languages. Accordingly, the Toronto Police Service has a number of available options for language interpretation. If a call from a non-English-speaking person is received at the Communications Services Unit, it is routed through Language Line Services, an organization that the Toronto Police Service has contracted with since 1991. More than 140 languages may be interpreted with this service. As well, police may use this service in a variety of situations, including arrest, rights to counsel, and ascertaining any medical needs. However, a member interpreter of the Service, registered with the Human Resources Management System, is used for statement taking or conducting further investigations. The Victim Services Program of Toronto, which is physically housed at the Toronto Police Service headquarters and available 24/7 to police personnel, can also assist individuals and families in crisis as staff and volunteers speak 30 languages.

Multilingual Community Interpreter Services (MCIS) is provincially mandated by the Ministry of Citizenship and Immigration in Ontario, to provide cultural interpretation for agencies, shelters, as well as government and police services for victims of sexual assaults and domestic violence or intimate abuse situations (M.C.I.S. Sukamar, 2006, personal communication). The Toronto Police Service has a contractual agreement with MCIS for cases of domestic violence and sexual assaults. Interestingly, this agency conducted research, including focus group sessions with police and other service providers, in consideration of an expansion of its services to other areas, including elder abuse. This initiative was enthusiastically commended in the elder abuse service providers' community. The MCIS *Giving Voice* report, which acknowledged the problems and challenges of language barriers in older ethnically diverse populations, as well as the great need for cultural interpretation services, has, disappointingly, been tabled. The organization continues to lobby at the provincial level for funding to serve this overlooked community (M.C.I.S. O'Donohue, 2008, personal communication).

The availability of cultural interpretation is also important to note, as the Greater Toronto Area has at least 24 recognized faiths (2001 Census). The City of Toronto makes the following statement on its Immigration and Settlement Portal. "Diversity is Toronto's strength. It is a city where you can meet people from more than 200 different countries, speaking 150 distinct languages" (http://www.toronto.ca/immigration/diversity_imm.htm). Given Toronto's increasingly aging and diverse population, this cultural interpretation service, from MCIS, would be of considerable valuable in elder abuse investigations.

L.E.A.P.S.

In 2003, a Greater Toronto Area police organization known as L.E.A.P.S. (Law Enforcement Agencies Protecting Seniors) was established. It subsequently expanded to south/central Ontario and now operates province-wide. Currently, it has a membership of 31 representing 13 police services, the Public Guardian and Trustee's Office, plus the Ontario Police College (OPC). The Ontario Police College, with the assistance of L.E.A.P.S. has successfully organized three elder abuse conferences in 2004, 2005, and 2006, with more planned. Members of L.E.A.P.S. optimistically work toward replacing these conferences with a specialized elder abuse investigations course at OPC. At present, the Ottawa Police Service offers the only stand-alone elder abuse investigators' course in the province.

Furthermore, as a result of a L.E.A.P.S. initiative, in late 2005, a comprehensive elder abuse training DVD was developed for police personnel through the Ontario Police Training Video Alliance (OPTVA). In early 2006, it was distributed to all police services across the province. Although it does not include information on all aspects of elder abuse, it is quite extensive. Greatly adding to its credibility, it includes introductory vignettes written and acted by the multitalented Joan Hill. Ms. Hill portrays a victim of elder abuse in various circumstances while police scenarios and expert commentary round out the training component of this educational tool.

Elder abuse coordinator

Since the mid-1990s, the Toronto Police Service has had an officer, in the role of Elder Abuse Co-Ordinator, dedicated to fulfilling administrative duties for both older and vulnerable adult abuse and neglect issues. Currently, an officer (the author of this chapter) holds these same responsibilities, as well as the mental health portfolio. As such, the duties of the officer responsible for Vulnerable Persons Issues encompasses the following: liaising with and assisting Service field units and other non-front-line units as an internal resource; assisting with the development of Service educational programs; providing Service training; reviewing, and updating appropriate Service procedures, as required; facilitating and enhancing communications between the Service and local service providers; liaising with other police services, government agencies, and community groups on initiatives or projects of mutual interest; developing partnerships; developing and maintaining a resource library; staying current with legislation and other matters pertaining to such issues; acting as a community referral resource; representing the interests of the Service while sitting on various committees; finally, engaging in public education and training on these topics.

Providing information to members of the Service is an important task in this officer's role. In Toronto, the *Policing a Diverse Community* course has been offered to both police and civilian personnel since 1997 through the Training and Education Unit. This course provides an overview of a variety of topics, including a component on older/vulnerable adult abuse and neglect issues. More recently, the *Crime Prevention* course for police personnel has added an elder abuse awareness segment.

Senior crime stoppers

For those members of the public who are reluctant to directly report on a crime or suspected criminal activity and subsequently identify themselves as complainants, there is an alternative method. Toronto Crime Stoppers, in partnership with Toronto Police Service has officially operated a "Senior Crime Stoppers" tip line since June 2001 (416-222-TIPS, http://www.222tips.com). Tips may be submitted via the telephone, by text, or online. Crime Stoppers guarantees anonymity and does not subscribe to caller ID. While it does not generate a large number of tips, it does nonetheless receive reports from the general public relating to offences involving older adults. Visit the website for information on the Senior Crime Stoppers program. The Toronto Police Service also offers community presentations on this program.

Ensuring all citizens in the province have this same opportunity, in January 2006, the Ministry of Community Safety and Correctional Services, through the Ontario Association of Crime Stoppers, launched Senior Crime Stoppers province-wide. An interactive, bilingual DVD was produced at the time and sent to all 39 local Crime Stoppers programs in the province to use in presentations to seniors groups. Seniors concerned about fraud, abuse, neglect and other crimes will learn how to protect themselves (Ministry of Community Safety and Correctional Services, 2006).

OACP resolution

In 2003, the Ontario Association of Chiefs of Police (OACP) publicly reaffirmed their commitment to Resolution 2003-01, *Vulnerable Adult Abuse*, passed at their annual meeting (Ontario Association of Chiefs of Police, 2003). This has led, in some police services across the province, to the recognition of elder abuse and neglect as an important emerging issue. This is in addition to what the Police Services Act, Regulation 3/99 "Adequacy and Effectiveness for Police Services" stipulates. Section 12 (1) states: "Every chief of police shall develop and maintain procedures on and processes for undertaking and managing general criminal investigations and investigations into, ... (f) elder abuse and vulnerable adult abuse ..." (http://www.e-laws.gov.on.ca/html/regs/english/elaws_regs_990003_e.htm).

Ontario's "strategy to combat elder abuse"

In 2002, the Ontario government responded to the issue of elder abuse and neglect with a pioneering, multiyear, multimillion dollar provincial strategy

(Ministry of Citizenship and Immigration – Ontario Seniors' Secretariat & Ministry of the Attorney General and Ontario Network for the Prevention of Elder Abuse (2003) http://www.culture.gov.on.ca/seniors/english/news/2006/b20060227.shtml). This three-pronged strategy, developed by the Ontario Seniors' Secretariat, focuses on (1) the coordination of community services, (2) training for front-line staff, and (3) public education to raise awareness. Partnering with the Ministry of the Attorney General's Victim Services Secretariat and the Ontario Network for the Prevention of Elder Abuse (ONPEA) to implement the strategy, it uses a holistic approach and recognizes stakeholders from several areas, including the legal and criminal justice sector. ONPEA originally received five-year funding for the strategy. In 2007, with additional monies from the Ontario government, this initiative was extended for two more years, till 2009.

In the summer of 2008, ONPEA partnered with Service Canada and in September of the same year delivered elder abuse awareness training to approximately 600 front-line and outreach staff from nearly 200 offices and outreach sites across the province. With this increased understanding and awareness of all types of elder abuse and neglect, Service Canada employees have the potential to assist more than 12 million Ontarians through this initiative, particularly as it relates to those accessing government programs and services. In April 2009, ONPEA announced the establishment of a province-wide elder abuse hot line telephone number (http://www.onpea.org/#). It provides both resources and assistance to older persons in abusive relationships in 150 languages and is available 24 hours a day, 7 days a week. Operating in conjunction with the Assaulted Women's Help Line, it is expected to support more than 500 older adults in its first year of operation (ONPEA, Kay, 2008, personal communication).

It should also be noted that since 2004, and pre-dating the launch on June 15, 2006 as World Elder Abuse Awareness Day by the International Network for Prevention of Elder Abuse, Ontario has designated October 19th as Elder Abuse Awareness Day. The province has also delivered annual elder abuse conferences in conjunction with the ONPEA.

Recommendations for justice practitioners

Police can sometimes face a complicated legal and ethical dilemma of when to become involved in an elder abuse case. It is important to understand that a capable senior, living an at-risk lifestyle or in an abusive situation, has the right to live life as he or she chooses and even refuse assistance. Older, capable persons have the right to self-determination. Unless the person is either in imminent physical danger or is mentally incapable, there may be nothing that can be done at that point in time.

While elder abuse is not solely the responsibility of the criminal justice system, it is up to justice practitioners to ensure that when an older adult abuse case is brought to their attention, it is given every consideration—from the initial report-taking, to the investigation through prosecution and sentencing.

Officers must change the way they do business. They must slow the process down, exercise patience, be sensitive to any special needs, build trust, and offer support. Officers must listen carefully, while speaking directly and privately with the older victim. No matter the outcome, suitable community supports must be offered, even repeatedly, to the victim.

During the course of the entire investigation, law enforcement personnel must consider the vulnerability of the victim. But, while doing so, they must also consider the victim's capabilities and be careful not to further disempower him or her. Officers need to be aware of their personal attitudes and biases and consider any and all systemic issues. They must consider all possible interventions and ensure community supports are in place, particularly if the victim is "at risk." It is also imperative that they suspend judgment about the case and work to develop an understanding of the context in which the behaviors are occurring.

If the matter proceeds to court, they should provide information to the victim about the law and the criminal justice system. This is critical, particularly if the abuser is a family member. Officers need to keep the victim updated regarding case status, arrest, charges, court dates, release conditions, and so on. If the victim is required to testify, an officer needs to explain the criminal court process and offer the appropriate court preparation. The officer must also consider such issues as the time of day the victim is expected to take the stand and how this may overlap with his or her medication schedule, mobility status, and access to transportation. All such considerations potentially impact the victim's ability to testify. The officer should also ensure that both the prosecutor and the judge are made aware that this case involves an elderly victim.

It is imperative that officers develop a sense of trust and understanding with the older victim. This can usually be accomplished by being considerate and respectful. As a professional, this is something the officer should already be doing. After the victim feels comfortable, determine who, if anyone, should be present during the interview process. Be patient and reassuring. Avoid unnecessary pressure. A recent study (Stevens et al., 2008) has suggested that older adults have more difficulty in concentrating on a task when there are distractions. This has obvious and important implications for the investigator. Some older persons may need time to collect their thoughts. Allow the victim to describe the incident in his or her own words. Consider statements from other family members, caregivers, or outside service providers. One of the most important things is for the victim to know who the investigating officer is and to have contact information.

Conclusion

What do victims of elder abuse want? Community Legal Education Ontario offers the following advice. Similar to all abusive relationships, they want the abuser to stop the violence, exploitation, or neglect. They need safe, suitable shelter, and access to financial resources. They require home support services so they are not dependent on the abuser to meet their needs. They also need emotional support, counseling, and appropriate links to the community for a healthy, abuse-free future. Finally, victims of elder abuse must be advised of all available options, including information about the law, the criminal justice system, and if they choose to proceed with a criminal investigation, the likely outcomes. This is imperative, particularly if the abuser is a family member.

This chapter has described gaps in the system, as well as some promising steps in bridging them. It is important to remember that as our world ages, so too do we as service providers, but perhaps, more significantly as community members. As a society, it behooves us to do well unto others, as we hope others will do for us in our older years. All told, "The mark of a noble society is found not in how it protects the powerful, but how it defends the vulnerable" (HelpAge International, 2000). These are commanding words indeed for justice practitioners.

References

Bond, J.B., Cuddy, R., Dixon, G.L., Duncan, K.A., Smith, D.L., 1999. The financial abuse of mentally incompetent older adults: a Canadian study. J. Elder Abuse Negl. 11 (4), 23–38.

Canadian Bankers Association, 2006. Safeguarding your money: a guide to protecting your money and resolving bank problems. <http://cba.ca/en/content/publications/Eng_Safeguarding_FINAL.pdf/>

Canadian Bankers Association, 2007. CBA Submission to House of Commons Standing Committee on Access to Information, Privacy and Ethics on Five Year Review of Personal Information Protection and Electronic Documents Act.

City of Toronto, 2006. Backgrounder: Release of the 2006 Census on Language, Immigration, Citizenship, Mobility/Migration. <http://www.toronto.ca/demographics/pdf/2006_lang_imm_citizenship_mobility_backgrounder.pdf/>

City of Toronto, undated. City of Toronto Immigration & Settlement Portal. <http://www.toronto.ca/immigration/diversity_imm.htm/>

Cohen, E.S., 2001. The complex nature of ageism: What is it? Who does it? Who perceives it? Gerontologist 41 (5), 575–577.

Department of Justice Canada, 2006. Personal information protection and electronic documents act. <http://www.privcom.gc.ca/legislation/02_06_01_e.asp/>

Financial Consumer Agency of Canada. <http://www.fcac-acfc.gc.ca/eng/publications/Tips-eng.asp/>

Health Canada, 1998. Principles of the National Framework on Aging: A Policy Guide (Cat. No. H88-3/21-1998E). Minister of Public Works and Government Services Canada, Ottawa, ON.

HelpAge International, 2000. The Mark of a Noble Society: Human Rights and Older People. HelpAge International, London, UK.

Martin's Annual Criminal Code, 2006 edition, 2006. Aurora, ON: Canada Law Book Inc. <http://laws.justice.gc.ca/en/showdoc/cs/C-46/bo-ga:l_XXIII-gb:s_718_21//en#anchorbo-ga:l_XXIII-gb:s_718_21/>

Ministry of the Attorney General, 2005. Crown Policy Manual. <www.attorneygen-eral.jus.gov.on.ca/english/crim/cpm/default.asp/>

Ministry of the Attorney General, April 3, 2006. Conversation with Lisa Jacek, Crown Lead, Elder Abuse Policy. Criminal Law Policy Branch. Toronto, ON.

Ministry of the Attorney General, April 18, 2006. Correspondence with Dimitra Tasagaris, Assistant Crown Attorney.

Ministry of the Attorney General, October 6, 2008. Conversation with Lisa Jacek, Crown Lead, Elder Abuse Policy. Criminal Law Policy Branch. Toronto, ON.

Ministry of Citizenship and Immigration. Seniors' Secretariat, Senior Smart Ontario, undated. Statistics on Ontario Seniors. <http://www.citizenship.gov.on.ca/seniors/english/seniorsmart-statistics.htm/>

Ministry of Citizenship and Immigration-Ontario Seniors' Secretariat, Ministry of the Attorney General and Ontario Network for the Prevention of Elder Abuse, June, 2003. Ontario's strategy to combat elder abuse, pamphlet, Toronto, ON: Government of Ontario.

Ministry of Citizenship and Immigration, Ontario Seniors' Secretariat, 2006. McGuinty government protecting Ontario's seniors—New funding enhances community services, helps combat elder abuse. News release, November 7. <http://www.citizenship.gov.on.ca/seniors/english/n030506.htm/>

Ministry of Community Safety and Correctional Services, R.S.O. 1990. *Police Services Act*, Ont. Reg. 3/99 Adequacy and Effectiveness of Police Service. <http://www.e-laws.gov.on.ca/html/regs/english/elaws_regs_990003_e.htm/>

Ministry of Community Safety and Correctional Services, 2006. Province promotes crime prevention for Ontario seniors. News release, January 25. <http://ogov.newswire.ca/ontario/GPOE/2006/01/25/c0400.html?lmatch=&lang=_e.html/>

Ministry of the Solicitor General, *LE-021*—Elder and vulnerable abuse2000. Policing Stand. Man. <http://www.mcscs.jus.gov.on.ca/english/police_serv/pol_stand.html/>

Multilingual Community Interpreter Service, 2006. <http://www.mcis.on.ca/>

Multilingual Community Interpreter Service, August 1, 2006. Correspondence with Latha Sukamar, Executive Director, MCIS. Toronto, ON.

Multilingual Community Interpreter Service, August 14, 2008. Conversation with Darlene O'Donohue, Director of Service Development and Customer Relations, MCIS. Toronto, ON.

Novak, M., Campbell, L., 2001. Aging and Society: A Canadian Perspective, fourth ed. Nelson Thompson Learning, Scarborough, ON.

Ontario Association of Chiefs of Police, 2003. Ontario police leaders demand action against elder abuse. Press release, September 18. <http://www.oacp.on.ca/content/news/article.html?ID=48/>

Ontario Association of Chiefs of Police, April 7, 2006. Conversation with Joe Couto, Director of Government Relations and Communications. Toronto, ON.

Ontario Association of Crime Stoppers, undated. Operational Guidelines and Appendices Manual. <http://www.ontariocrimestoppers.com/manual.htm/>

Ontario Network for the Prevention of Elder Abuse, August 25, 2008. Conversation with Teri Kay, Executive Director. Toronto, ON. <http://www.onpea.org/en/index.html/>

Payne, D., Berg, B., Toussaint, J., 2001. The police response to the criminalization of elder abuse: an exploratory study. Policing 24 (4), 605–625.

Podnieks, E., Pillemer, K., Nicholson, J.P., Shillington, P., Frizell, A., 1990. National Survey on Abuse of the Elderly in Canada. The Ryerson Study. Ryerson Polytechnical Institute, Toronto, ON.

Province of Ontario. Police Services Act, Ontario. Regulation 3/99, Adequacy and Effectiveness of Police Services. <http://www.e-laws.gov.on.ca/html/regs/english/elaws_regs_ 990003_e.htm/>

Province of Ontario, 2008. What You Need to Know About Elder Abuse [fact sheet]. Ontario Senior Secretariat, Toronto, ON Retrieved July 25, 2008 from <http://www.culture.gov.on.ca/seniors/english/programs/elderabuse/docs/needtoknow.pdf/>.

Statistics Canada, 2001. Seniors in Canada. Canadian Centre for Justice Statistics Profile Series Catalogue no. 85F0033MIE.

Statistics Canada, 2001. 2001 Community Profiles.

Stevens, W.D., Hasher, L., Chiew, K.S., Grady, C.L., 2008. A neural mechanism underlying memory failure in older adults. J. Neurosci. 28 (48), 12820–12824 doi:10.1523/JNEUROSCI.2622-08.2008.

Toronto Crime Stoppers. <http://www.222tips.com/index.php/>

Toronto Police Service, 2000. Procedure 05-22, Abuse of Elderly or Vulnerable Persons. TPS, Toronto, ON.

Toronto Police Service, March 12, 2002. 2005 Environmental Scan. TPS, Toronto, ON. < http://www.torontopolice.on.ca/publications/files/reports/2005envscan.pdf>

Toronto Police Service, 2006a. 2006–2008 Business Plan. TPS, Toronto, ON.

Toronto Police Service, 2006b. TPS 2005 Statistical Report. TPS, Toronto, ON. <www.torontopolice.on.ca/publications/files/reports/2005statsreport.pdf>

Trevitt, C., Gallagher, E., 1996. Elder abuse in Canada and Australia: implications for nurses. Int. J. Nurs. Stud. 33 (6), 651–659.

United Nations, 1991. Principles for older persons. Resolution 46/9/16 December. <http://www.un.org/NewLinks/older/99/principles.htm/>

United Nations, October 16, 1992. Proclamation on ageing. <http://www.un.org/documents/ga/res/47/a47r005.htm/>

United Nations, 2002. Valencia Forum Statement. <http://www.un.org/swaa2002/coverage/vforumE.htm/>

United Nations, 2007. World population prospects: the 2006 revision, Executive summary. <http://www.un.org/esa/population/publications/wpp2006/English.pdf/>

Wahl, J., 2008. Elder Abuse: The Hidden Crime. Community Legal Education Ontario. http://www.cleo.on.ca/english/pub/onpub/PDF/seniors/elderab.pdf/>

WHO/INPEA, 2002. Missing Voices: Views of Older Persons on Elder Abuse. World Health Organization, Geneva.

7 Seneca College's design for social change course: an example of successful collaboration

Paul Shecter, Patricia Fleischmann

The first class

It is just before 9 a.m. on an early January day in 2006. The students slowly file into the classroom for the first session of their capstone course in the Seneca College Communication Design Program titled Design for Social Change (DFSC). Rumor has it that the project they will undertake in this course will be difficult and time consuming. In fact, it will consume about 230 hours, which over the 7 weeks of the course, works out to about 33 hours a week, a full-time job's commitment for students who are also enrolled in other classes. The DFSC projects are for "real" clients who change each time the course is run, therefore, the students' usually reliable grapevine can't help them know what lies ahead. They wait and wonder.

There are four preparatory readings, including the *First Things First Manifesto 2000*, originally written by Ken Garland in 1964.* Its theme is that designers should not focus solely on the commercial by promoting products. It suggests they should also aspire to loftier goals and use their skills to promote better community life. In many ways, this and the other preparatory readings disparage the curriculum the students have been studying for the past five semesters. For example, Jorge Frascara's (2001) article discusses four categories of design; but the only one they have previously been exposed to is what he calls "inconsequential design," design that promotes one product over another. One purpose for assigning these readings is to lead the students to question why, for the five previous semesters, they have focused on packaging and other aspects of commercial design. A second purpose is to introduce them to prominent designers who question the commercially skewed priorities of a large segment of the design industry.

The students have been promised a quiz on the readings on this first day of class. It is a hard quiz, composed mostly of short essay questions and their

---

*First Things First Manifesto 2000, an update version of the 1964 document, signed by 33 graphic designers, art directors and visual communicators, was published in *Adbusters Magazine* (Autumn, 1998, p. 22), *Emigre Magazine* (1999, v. 51), and many other magazines around the world targeted to the design community.

guest speaker is waiting. After the quiz, the guest, a marketing expert, begins to talk about different types of marketing used to sell products. He reviews the four basic "P's" of marketing: Price, Product, Placement, and Promotion and discusses key motivating factors that influence the consumer. An interactive discussion of branding follows. After this, he switches gears and begins to explain social marketing, illustrating differences and similarities between it and product marketing. To the four "P's" of marketing, social marketing adds a fifth "P," and that is People. Social marketing is about changing behavior. The students are told that if a campaign asks people to give something up, something else of equal or greater value must be offered to replace it. The P that stands for Price becomes Participation.

At the end of the day, the students ask what their homework is and are told to review their notes and readings. The client will be at the next class, and they should not be late. But what is the project?

Objective of this chapter

Although elder abuse and ageism were the topics of the project, this chapter does not attempt to define, discuss, or elaborate on either as social constructs. Instead, the objective is to describe a college course that produces successful social marketing campaigns. Hopefully, NGOs and other organizations in the field of elder abuse prevention and other socially relevant issues can learn from this example how a change in their approach to the communication design industry could lead to more effective social marketing campaigns.

The evolution of the design for social change course

Following a three-decade career as a practicing Graphic Designer, this chapter's first author made a mid-life decision to learn to teach his trade. After completion of the required Masters degree, which involved several years of part-time teaching, he assumed his first full-time university teaching position at a satellite campus of the University of Wisconsin in Platteville, Wisconsin. Graphic Design there was a small segment of the Fine Art Department, and he was the only faculty member who specialized in design. To prepare his students for careers in design, he knew that they needed more varied training/mentoring than any one professor could provide, and he conceived of a way to involve them with other faculty: a mini design studio course. It received approval from the other departments and the University and in 1999 was offered for the first time to marketing students, design students, and print/web production students. The basic concept was to try to emulate a working studio and take on "real" projects, initially campus poster projects. Then, a bit of serendipity brought a real public service client into the fledgling studio course. Wisconsin has a state policy that encourages publicly funded colleges to take on projects that give back to the state.

In this context, Rick Fujita, Communications Director at Platteville was asked by the State of Wisconsin, Department of Labor Relations for help with a project. The project had the goal of generating increased awareness, interest, and use of the State's employee suggestion program. As his office was overloaded at the time, he asked if the graphics design studio course would tackle the project. It was enthusiastically received by the whole team. Before suggesting changes to the program's procedures, the students interviewed end users to find out why the previous system was difficult to use. After receiving approval for their suggested procedural changes from the Department of Labor Relations, they designed posters, brochures, and web pages to publicize the changes. The campaign was a success. It was implemented by the State of Wisconsin, and the team members received kudos from the Governor.

In 2001, after a move to Seneca College in Toronto, Professor Shecter was asked by Lauretta Wood, the Graphic Design Program Coordinator, to design an exit course for the graduating students that would make use of all of the skills and theory they had acquired during their previous five semesters. This opportunity allowed him to develop and expand the concept that he had originated in Wisconsin. Seneca classes were much larger, and he decided to divide each class into work groups that emulated design studio teams. Their projects would be chosen to allow them to see the effect of their design work in their own community. It was fortunate that as well as the coordinator, the chair of the School of Communication Arts and the dean of Information Arts at Seneca saw the potential of interaction between design students and social marketing campaigns. All were supportive of this unique program.

Projects brought to the course

Projects that clients have brought to the course at Seneca include the promotion of a non-judgmental exit program for young prostitutes (linked to a campaign to discourage the use of prostitution) and information campaigns to promote awareness of: a hot line for delinquents under 12 years of age; child abuse issues (Toronto Police Service, 2009); and of the early warning signs of intimate partner violence (RGD Ontario, 2006; Seneca College Media Relations, 2006). However the project that is the focus of this chapter was about elder abuse and ageism. It was brought to Seneca by Constable Patricia Fleischmann of the Community Mobilization Unit, Toronto Police Service.

Purposes of the course

The technical purposes of the course are to allow the students to put into play what they have learned in earlier semesters to expose them to a real-life client and designer–client interaction. They also learn about "bottom-up research" and usability testing methods that are effective tools for studying sociologically based design problems. The course's overarching and unifying principal, however, is to develop the students' awareness of the potential for their design skills to improve the lives of citizens in their own communities. This sense of purpose had been critical to the success of all the campaigns done thus far; the students became involved in the subject matter of their campaign. They were not given predefined solutions and asked to use their design skills to execute someone else's concept, thus they became personally immersed in the social issues that created the problems.

Role of the client

What gets 20-year-old students who are eager to graduate concerned about and inspired to work on complex social issues such as elder abuse and ageism? A large part of the answer lies in the role of the client. Before the first class ever meets, potential clients are briefed about their role as both facilitators of the students' research and as an ongoing participant in the class as a consultant. They are cautioned not to impose their solutions on the students if they want truly inspired work to emerge.

In the DFSC class, a primary role of the client is to help supply the experts, the background information and the contextual knowledge that will assist the students in defining the problem. For the campaign about elder abuse and ageism, Constable Fleischmann was an ideal client. Once discussions got underway, she initiated contact with a number of recognized leaders in the elder abuse community in Toronto who could offer specific and varied perspectives on the topic. These included Judith Wahl, Executive Director of the Advocacy Centre for the Elderly (ACE); Bill Gleberzon, Co-Director of Government and Media Relations for Canada's Association for the Fifty-Plus (CARP); Jeff Poirrier, Manager of Communications and Education in the Policy and Education Branch at the Ontario Human Rights Commission; Paula David, Coordinator of the Holocaust Resource Project at Baycrest Centre for Geriatric Care; Dr Elizabeth Podnieks, Honorary Chair of the Board of Directors for the Ontario Network for the Prevention of Elder Abuse (ONPEA); and Dr Lisa Manuel, Manager of Seniors and Caregivers Support Services of the Family Service Association of Toronto.

When Constable Fleischmann began participating in the class, she did not have a clear idea how to use imagery to combat elder abuse or ageism, but she did know what types of posters she had previously seen that did not resonate with the target audience. She also knew she did not want a campaign that evoked pity or, given Toronto's rich cultural diversity, that spoke to only one ethnic group.

Constable Fleischmann's first dilemma was how to introduce the topic to the class. What should be said? What would have the biggest impact? Being cognizant that this was a class of young adults, she knew that the introduction she was developing must resonate with youth. After discussions with a colleague who had worked with another group of Professor Shecter's students on a domestic violence campaign in 2005, she assembled a diverse collection of still photographs of older adults who were in distress, who had been victimized, neglected, or abused and presented them at the same time as Nat King Cole's song "Oh, What a Wonderful World." Both the music and photographs were available on the Internet, and for copyright reasons they were played simultaneously. The result of juxtaposing the pictures and music was obvious. For these anguished individuals, the world was anything but wonderful.

It was a mesmerizing opening. Without a single world being spoken, based on the students' emotional reactions and their body language, it was apparent that the music and images made a fitting prelude to the class discussion of elder abuse and the upcoming campaign. Professor Shecter explained that the goal of the elder abuse campaign was first to increase public awareness and understanding, and secondly, to change thoughts, attitudes, and behaviors toward the elderly. His brief introduction was followed by a series of presentations by professionals whose work related to the multifaceted problems of ageism and elder abuse. Constable Fleischmann spoke first and introduced the criminal justice perspective. The next stakeholder presentation, on the role of culture in elder abuse, was by Monita Persaud, the Multi-cultural Coordinator for the ONPEA. Bill Gleberzon, Co-Director, Government and Media Relations of CARP followed with a talk on respect, empowerment, and valuing of older adults.

At the next class, Constable Fleischmann provided an overview from a law enforcement point of view, of two neglect cases that had received considerable media attention. Paula David, from Baycrest Centre for Geriatric Care then discussed the aging process and gender differences in older adults. An older woman, associated with Ms. David through Baycrest, took the stage next. "Sally" was a remarkable speaker. As a mature woman, she recounted her life experiences and talked about the numerous challenges of aging. She spoke of her relationships with her own children. She told the students about her friends and their lives. She talked about good, as well as bad relationships and the impacts of these associations on older people. This particular session was riveting. "Sally's" contribution to this project cannot be overstated. Her frank and earnest discourse on the trials and tribulations of aging and her thoughts on abuse were the single most important features in the development of this elder abuse awareness campaign. On countless occasions, students in the class conveyed how she impacted their lives. They were able to personally relate "Sally's" message to their own immediate and extended families. Their own experiences took on new meaning as they reflected upon her words. "Sally" was a real, albeit older, person. She was someone who could not be ignored and who caused students to self-ruminate in ways never contemplated. It was a notable example of cause and effect.

Wrapping up the class after "Sally" was the Communications and Public Education Manager for the Ontario Human Rights Commission, Jeff Poirier, who discussed elder abuse, ageism, and age discrimination as human rights issues. The final presentation was by Judith Wahl, the Executive Director of the ACE, a Toronto-based community legal aid clinic for low-income seniors.

Ms. Wahl described the role of ACE in providing legal assistance to older adults. As well, she shared her professional know-how on responding to and dealing with older adults in need.

Two key themes emerged from the stakeholders' presentations. One was the lack of respect shown the elderly, while the other was that discrimination is often based solely on age. The students clearly got the message that abuse of older people is wrong, yet not one of their campaigns focused on the negatives. As shown in Figures 1–9, they chose instead to promote respect and to point out the unjust effects of ageism.

Contrast between some typical agency procedures and the DFSC class procedures

Social marketing clients often approach a studio and present their issue in a brief that explains the purpose of their organization in broad terms. They may also provide the studio some recent detailed research reports germane to the issue they want addressed in a campaign. However, social issues are often viewed as common knowledge, and studio teams are viewed as communications experts, therefore, in the initial dialogue, it tends to be assumed that the communication experts will find the focal issue to communicate to the "general public." Clients leave their brief and wait for the studio to contact them,

Figure 1

Figure 2

but the process often becomes stalled. Eventually there is a set of round robin meetings seeking a solution; a compromise may be reached. But far too often, both the studio and the client feel frustrated, and they have a campaign that only partially addresses the issue.

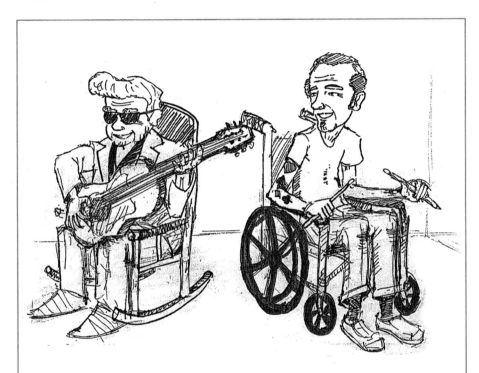

We invented "Rock & Roll"

You have more in common with your elders than you think. Hang out with them or just call. Find out what you're missing.

for more information visit: www.onpea.org

 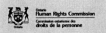

Seneca   Ontario Human Rights Commission / Commission ontarienne des droits de la personne   **CARP**

Figure 3

When we say "hip" we mean cool not replacement

You have more in common with your elders than you think. Hang out with them or just call. Find out what you're missing.

for more information visit: www.onpea.org

Seneca 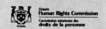 **CARP**

Figure 4

Two major differences between the studio procedure just described and the DFSC course are the bottom-up research that is undertaken by the students and the inclusion of the client as a facilitator throughout the research and design phases.

Maybe it's not Charlie
who needs to wear the glasses.

Contrary to popular beliefs,
Charlie is not senile or demented.
*Whether you see it or not, negative attitudes
towards seniors lead to elder abuse.*

*Help keep
our seniors safe.*

  CARP Ontario Human Rights Commission Commission ontarienne des droits de la personne   **Seneca**

Figure 5

A Typical.

Q What do you call a woman over
   65 who still looks after herself?

Respect our elders.
Respect ourselves.

  CARP  **Seneca**

Figure 6

Figure 7

Figure 8

Figure 9

The "bottom-up" research phase

As mentioned earlier, the students were asked to engage in "bottom-up" research. This type of research looks at all the data and tries to identify common threads. It is a form of qualitative research that is not controlled by a research question or statistical procedure. It is based on observation and incorporates many real-life variables, even when they seem conflicting. The students are taken through a series of exercises designed to help them broaden their investigation. In the second week of classes, they learn to write a questionnaire and go into the field to collect interview data. In the third week, they engage in an in-class exercise designed to help them discover key words and ideas that describe the influences spoken about by the client, in the stakeholder presentations, and during the interviews. Using dictionaries and thesauri, each group is asked to choose, for each letter of the alphabet, at least five words that resonate with the topic. If some groups do not understand the procedure, Professor Shecter leads the exercise as a class-as-a-whole oral activity. This brings up another hurdle—learning to cooperate. Sometimes students with good ideas don't want to share them for fear they will be stolen. Remember, these students have just experienced five semesters of competitive, commercially focused training. The idea of team creativity was very unfamiliar. But after working cooperatively on this exercise, they usually discover that there are enough aspects of a social marketing topic (and therefore enough good concepts to develop) for each group to have a unique theme that will speak to the target audience.

In the next research exercise, the groups conjure up images based on their word lists. When they have both word lists and an image file, a copywriter comes to class to help them with copy concepts, especially headlines that will complement or supplement their image ideas and image words. The last exercise the copywriter does with the students is to work on words that emote and provide a "call to action" for their concepts. Then, they are ready to produce a first draft of their concepts that they will take back to a small sample of the target audience for feedback (a usability test).

During the elder abuse/ageism project, a perfect opportunity for a field test of our work presented itself when a group of film broadcast students came into the class to tape an interview with the design students, about a strike that had just ended. When the visitors noticed the work-ups of our campaigns on the wall, the tables were turned, and the design students interviewed the broadcast crew about the meaning of the posters. The result: what was ageism? The media students could not define it. For the groups working on the project, this was a real eye opener. They learned that after the client's and stakeholders' presentations, they were no longer the typical consumer regarding this topic. Because the term *ageism* was not understood by other college-age students, it had to be replaced in their campaigns with words and images that defined it. Prior to this incident, most of the projects had used the term ageism, assuming it would be widely understood.

Client's role as facilitator

The client is the real expert on the topic of each campaign. From the first pre-planning session onward, an effort is made to get the client to talk and to get everyone else to listen. The students need to be immersed in the client's issue for seven weeks. To do this, the client chooses who to bring to the class, the number of experts, and what supplementary materials the students should be exposed to. There is extensive discussion between the client and the professor about how, working together, they can make the needs of the target audience understood by 20-year-old students. Where can more information be found? What hand-outs do the experts have that they can leave with the students? And most importantly, how many classes can the client/facilitator come to? Can they entice their "expert stakeholders" to come a second time during the process to see how the students are progressing and to offer feedback? Finally, it is necessary for every-one involved to commit a day to viewing and reviewing the final presentations. At the end of seven weeks, some of the students' work is still conceptual. They may not yet have flushed out, finished campaigns. But from their concepts, with the benefit of knowledgeable critique, final campaigns can be polished, pro-duced, and later distributed. Again, Constable Fleischmann was an ideal client. She came to class every week and supported both the instructor and the stu-dents. Sometimes, she was specifically asked for an opinion. Other times, she commented without solicitation, providing constructive feedback and stimulat-ing the teams to think about the issues from different viewpoints. These sessions were invaluable as students and client connected; she participating in an effective but unobtrusive way while learning about the design process.

Who owns the final projects? What has happened to them?

The final design copyright is jointly owned by Seneca College and the student designers. The Toronto Police Service has unlimited usage rights to the students' work. The service is thus able to and has incorporated this campaign into displays and presentations by police personnel. The work has also been pre-sented at several conferences including the ONPEA annual elder abuse con-ference held in Toronto in February 2006 attended by more than 500 people, and the 16th Annual John K. Friesen Conference held in May, 2006 at Simon Fraser University in British Columbia. The project has also been featured in a Toronto Police Service (2006a) publication (*The Badge*, March 2006) and on its website ("Elder abuse given voice"; Toronto Police Service, March 2006b), and it was the subject of a story on CARP's website as well ("Seneca students promote elder abuse awareness," 2006). Perhaps the most gratifying public display to date, however, was a joint initiative of the Toronto Police Service, ONPEA, the Ontario Senior's Secretariat, and the Ontario Victim Services Secretariat that developed one of the DFSC projects into a bilingual black and white poster. Titled "The One Abuse That No One Sees" (see Figure 10), it

Figure 10

Figure 11

was publicly shown for the first time on October 19, 2006, which has now been officially designated Ontario Elder Abuse Awareness Day. Subsequently, the posters were distributed province-wide. Another student project incorporated into the October 19 event were large, colorful "Flaunt Your Seniority" buttons (see Figure 11). They convey a positive message by encouraging seniors to feel pride and self-acceptance. In June 2008, Constable Fleischmann spoke to an international audience about this joint Toronto Police Service and Seneca College project at the International Network for Prevention of Elder Abuse's official World Elder Abuse Awareness Day event in Ottawa, Ontario.

Conclusion

The basis of social marketing is to do no harm and to change attitudes one person at a time by replacing negative behavior with something of equal or greater value. The immediate impact of these elder abuse awareness campaigns has been positive. After viewing them, people have stated that their appreciation of the complex issues of older adult abuse and neglect have become more sharply attuned. For some, it has forced an acknowledgement of the existence of elder abuse, and for others, it has allowed introspection of their own and others' ageist biases. The students reported feeling changed; so did the client. It is our impression that the DFSC course and its products can serve as a valuable model for others around the world combating elder abuse as well as neglect and the ageism that underpins these problematic behaviors.

References

Canada's Association for the Fifty-Plus, 2006. Seneca students promote elder abuse awareness. <http://www.carp.ca/article_display.cfm?documentID=1906&CabinetID=263&LibraryID=70&cityID=7>

Frascara, J., 2001. A history of design, a history of concerns. In: Heller, S., Ballance, G. (Eds.), Graphic Design History. Allworth Press, New York, NY, pp. 13–18.

Garland, K., 1964. First Things First Manifesto. Goodwin Press, London.

RGD Ontario, 2006. Seneca college partnership with Toronto Police Service. Retrieved August 2, 2008 from the website of the Association of Registered Graphic Designers of Ontario. <http://www.rgdontario.com/contentmanager/ViewObject. aspx?sys-Portal=38&sys-Class=Item&sys-ID=208>

Seneca College Media Relations, 2006. Seneca students' artwork shown larger than life at Rogers Centre. Press release August 22, 2003. Retrieved August 2, 2008 from Seneca college website. <http://www.senecac.on.ca/cms/media/newsdetail. jsp?mediaID=68>

Toronto Police Service, March, 2006a. Graphic combat of elder abuse. *The Badge.*

Toronto Police Service, March 6, 2006b. Elder abuse given voice. <http://www.chq. mtp.gov/tpsnet/stories/2006/2006.03.06-elderabuse/index.html>

Toronto Police Service, 2009. Partnering with Crime Stoppers. <http://www.torontopolice. on.ca/communitymobilization/domesticviolence/>

LaVergne, TN USA
22 May 2010
183543LV00002B/1/P